Everything you ever wanted to know about wind turbines for domestic power, but were afraid to ask

How to design & build your own domestic free energy solution

By

P Xavier BSc MSc

Copyright © 2018

ISBN 9781096678915

Introduction

Having read a number of books that claim to teach the reader how to build/install a PV/wind turbine installation, it became plainly obvious that they all fell into two camps. The first were written by science boffins & are packed with PhD level scientific formulae, which is way beyond the needs or ability of most DIYers. The second set was so brief & contained so little information that they were basically pamphlets padded out with useless & sometimes dangerous information. Neither of these can be of use to the average person. This book is therefore aimed at everyone & imparts practical information to anyone who wishes to learn about the practicalities & economics of installing, running & maintaining a home wind turbine system. It's not a guide for idiots, but a useful & practical guide for everyone.

This book contains the sections that are relevant to wind turbines from the book 'DIY home energy solutions' by the same author, where photovoltaic systems, wind turbine energy generating systems, back-up electricity systems, solar water heating, ground sourced hot water & also light tubes are covered in detail. Each of those topic areas have been arranged into three broad groups. Design, installation & also maintenance.

Therefore, the reader should become competent in designing, constructing & running a system that is suitable for their own unique & individual needs. Both here & in 'DIY home energy solutions' all areas have been laid out in plain & simple English, allowing the concepts to be within anyone's grasp, regardless of their academic ability.

Table of Contents

INTRODUCTION 2

TABLE OF CONTENTS 3

NOTES 6

CHAPTER 1 - WHOLESALE ENERGY USE & PRICE 7

CHAPTER 2 - THE COMPONENTS USED IN EVERY SYSTEM 10
- THE CONCEPT IN A NUTSHELL 10
- THE SYSTEM COMPONENTS 11
  - *Collection elements:* 11
  - *Control elements:* 12
  - *Store/Supply element:* 12
- CAN THIS POWER THE WORLD? 13

CHAPTER 3 - SOME NOTES ON ELECTRICITY 14
  - *Ohm's law* 15

CHAPTER 4 - WIND TURBINES 21
- WHERE DOES WIND COME FROM? 21
  - *The wind speed scale* 25
- TYPES OF WIND TURBINE 26
  - *Horizontal axis wind turbines (HAWT)* 26
  - *HAWT advantages* 28
  - *HAWT disadvantages* 28
  - *Anatomy of HAWT* 29
  - *Vertical axis wind turbines (VAWT)* 30
  - *VAWT advantages* 30
  - *VAWT disadvantages* 31
  - *Darrieus wind turbine* 32
  - *H-rotor gyromill wind turbine* 33
  - *Helical Darrieus wind turbine* 34
  - *Anatomy of VAWT* 35
- HOW A TURBINE TURNS IN THE WIND 35
  - *Air density* 37
  - *Rotor area* 38
  - *Wind turbines deflect the wind* 38
  - *Air pressure distribution in front & behind the rotor blades* 40
  - *The power of wind* 41

  Rooftop power *43*
  Orography *45*
  A convenient way to measure wind speed *47*
  Turbine noise *47*
 CALCULATING THE SOUND LEVEL EXPECTED FROM THE TURBINE 50
  Flicker *51*
 CHOOSING A MOUNT 51
  Guyed towers *53*
  Freestanding towers *55*
  Tower selection *56*
 PERSONAL POWER, NATIONAL GRID OR BOTH? 57
 FULMINOLOGY 57
  Protection for PV system *59*
  Protection for the wind turbine system *61*

CHAPTER 5 - CABLE MANAGEMENT 71
 BACK UP POWER 73

CHAPTER 6 - LEGISLATION IN THE UK 77
 PLANNING PERMISSION 77
  Domestic stand alone wind turbines *77*
  Building mounted wind turbines *79*
  Scotland, Wales & Northern Ireland *80*
 THE BUILDING REGULATIONS – WIND TURBINES 81
  Stand alone wind turbines *81*
  Building mounted wind turbines *82*
 BRITISH STANDARDS 82
  BS7671:2008 & Amendment 3 (2015) *82*
 FURTHER READING ON LEGISLATION 83

CHAPTER 7 - THE SYSTEM DESIGN 85
  Calculating your load *86*
  System costs *90*
  Payback *91*

CHAPTER 8 - MAINTENANCE 93
  Wind turbine maintenance *93*

CHAPTER 9 - USING A CALCULATOR TO DO THE MATHS 102

CHAPTER 10 - EASING THE INSTALLATION 105

CHAPTER 11 – OBTAINING FINANCE, GRANTS & MORTGAGES 110
 HIDDEN BENEFITS FROM USING A CPS INSTALLER 110
  Renewable Heat Incentive (RHI) *112*
 FURTHER GRANTS 114
  Grants for wind turbines *114*

MORTGAGES 117
    How mortgages can be affected by a wind turbine............................ 117

TABLE OF ILLUSTRATIONS.. **119**

INDEX **121**

ABOUT THE AUTHOR **127**

Notes

This work is by the author & as such, all copyright belongs to the author. You are not permitted to copy any text or images without the authors express permission.

Some of the images in this book are created by the book's author, others are either in the public domain or individually credited to their respective creator &/or copyright owner. Any other images are from sources where they are copyright free.

This work is fully referenced to aid the reader in any future studies. That being said, internet references have been provided to aid study as most individuals do not have huge libraries at their disposal. It is far easier to research material online than to go through the expense of ordering specific books at a public lending library.

Chapter 1 - Wholesale energy use & price

Everyone & everything in the developed world needs & uses electrical energy. Every home has electrical appliances that use electricity; therefore every household faces a sizeable annual bill for their energy use.

No doubt, most households have washing machines, fridge freezers, televisions, radios, computers, phones, DVD players, satellite receivers, hi-fi's, microwave ovens, alarm clocks, lighting, heating. The list goes on & on. Yet, using each & every one of these appliances costs money to run & this cost is set to rise year on year as fossil fuels are slowly depleted & demand for electricity rises.

Whilst demand for fossil fuels increases, so too will the cost. It is a simple case of demand outstripping supply which causes this monetary increase in costs.

In the UK, the 'National Grid' predicts the cost of electricity to double by 2035 & gas to rise by 33% over the same time period. This is due to various factors, depletion of fossil fuels, governmental 'green energy incentives', lack of investment & most telling, the fact that by 2035, the UK is predicted to need to import 90% of its energy needs[1].

In addition, the US Energy Information Administration (EIA) also predicts an increase of 48% in total world energy demand by 2040[2].

---

[1] https://www.theguardian.com/environment/2014/jul/10/price-electricity-double-next-20-years-national-grid - 28/08/2017

[2] https://www.eia.gov/todayinenergy/detail.php?id=26212 – 28/08/2017

The cost of obtaining energy has also risen 20% since 2009 & will clearly continue to increase; it therefore makes fiscal sense for all households to source as much energy as possible from cheaper alternatives. In addition to rising prices, the likelihood of future power cuts also increases dramatically.

The UK's Big Infrastructure Group (BIG) has warned that in the UK, the spare capacity of electrical energy that was ready to be delivered to consumers has fallen sharply in recent years. In 2011 - 2012 it was 17%, whilst in 2016 - 2017 it had fallen to 1%, therefore increasing the likelihood of blackouts[3]. BIG are not alone in predicting blackouts in the UK, the Institute of Mechanical Engineers predict that the UK will only have half the energy it needs by 2025 & they have also stated that "The UK is facing an electricity supply crisis"[4].

Since these predictions were made, both the UK & the EEC have announced that they intend to legislate to outlaw the sale of all new diesel & petrol vehicles by 2040[5]. The Green Alliance has stated that the UK grid is not ready for the anticipated demand that electric vehicles will place on the grid & that blackouts will occur as a result because it takes the same amount of electricity that an average household uses in three days to charge one electric car overnight[6].

They add that by 2025, 700,000 UK consumers will be experiencing blackouts due to this level of demand & also because of damage caused by increased levels of strain on the UK network. The UK electricity network was never designed to cope with these rising levels of predicted loads.

---

[3] https://www.rt.com/uk/370735-blackout-electricty-bills-rise/ - 28/08/2017

[4] https://theenergyst.com/uk-facing-power-blackouts-engineers-warn/ - 28/08/2017

[5] https://www.ft.com/content/7e61d3ae-718e-11e7-93ff-99f383b09ff9 - 09/09/2017

[6] https://www.theguardian.com/business/2017/apr/20/uk-unprepared-for-surge-in-electric-car-use-thinktank-warns - 09/09/2017

Luckily, the green energy brigade has been busy developing viable solutions for the energy market. Photovoltaic cells have halved in cost since 2008 & seen an overall 100% reduction in price since 1977[7]. In that time battery technology has also increased whilst the costs have decreased. The cost of batteries are predicted to continue to reduce in cost whilst the costs of fossil fuels increase[8]. It is predicted that there should be a further 70% decrease in battery costs by 2050. There are many energy companies currently researching battery technology which is being funded by car manufacturers, mobile phone companies & many others. Therefore it can be clearly seen that whilst there will be an incremental cost increase on domestic electricity, the cost of renewable energy solutions are set to plummet.

The sun & wind are currently free resources. They will remain to be a free resource until the government decides to levy a tax on them. Until that time, these free energy sources should be exploited to the fullest.

Therefore, the next logical step would be to look at the individual components that make up the installations that have the potential to save every household real money & thereby act as an investment, saving money for many years.

---

[7] https://cleantechnica.com/2014/02/04/current-cost-solar-panels/ - 28/08/2017

[8] https://cleantechnica.com/2014/10/20/grid-defection-makes-economic-sense/ - 28/08.2017

Chapter 2 - The components used in every system

All installations follow the same basic design principles as they are all made from the same basic components & operate in the same way. The only difference between any given system is the size & complexity of the individual elements. For instance, one system may have 20 batteries, another 200. One may have 4 photovoltaic panels, another may have 40. One may store energy on site to be used by the homeowner; another may opt to sell the electricity directly to the 'National Grid'.

There is no single correct solution to any given installation, but there are always better options to consider when undertaking the design. Cost for most will be a major factor when selecting individual components as these systems are an expensive investment. However, as previously stated, the costs are predicted to reduce significantly over the coming years.

The concept in a nutshell

Every system collects energy, transforms it into a useable form & then makes it available for the user. None of these systems create electricity; they just transform one form of energy into another (solar energy & kinetic energy into electricity). This is all due to one fundamental law of nature: energy cannot be destroyed, but it can move from one form to another.

This is a system that everyone is familiar with. For instance, as a tree grows it collects solar energy & converts it into sugar to fuel its life systems. It also stores some of that energy within its trunk, branches & leaves.

It has transformed solar energy into a form of energy that is more useful for it to use. We also can convert it into a form of energy that is more useful to us by simply burning the tree, thereby transforming the energy that the tree has stored into heat energy & a little back into light energy.

Another example could be: plants harness solar energy & convert it into sugar to fuel its life systems. It also stores some of that energy within its self, animals (including humans) eat the plants & use what the plants have made, to fuel themselves. It's not magic; it is just harnessing what nature does for our own benefit. Nature has been doing it for millions of years as it is so efficient. Harnessing solar & kinetic energy (solar & wind power) is just another method that we can harness for our needs.

The system components

As stated previously, all systems consist of the same basic components. They are as follows:

Collection elements:

Photovoltaic (PV) cells – these collect solar energy & convert it to useable electricity.

Wind turbines – these collect wind (kinetic) energy & convert it to useable electricity. The easiest way of understanding it, is by imagining a battery powered hand fan. Instead of the battery powering a motor that spins the blades to move the air, these wind turbines blades are turned by the wind & that energy is converted into electricity. It is the same principle of the hand fan, but bigger & working in reverse.

Water turbines (aka water wheel) – these collect water (kinetic) energy & convert it to useable electricity.

They work in exactly the same way as a wind turbine, but use moving water rather than moving wind. Water turbines are beyond the scope of this book as very few people have a suitable water source in their back gardens.

Control elements:

Charge controller – this acts as a buffer between the collection elements & the batteries. It is a clever piece of electronics that regulates the supply so that the batteries are protected from any electrical charge that could damage the batteries.

Inverter – this inverts the batteries DC output into AC output. Here in the UK & Europe, the nation's supply is 230v AC; in the USA they have 110v DC. It is therefore important to know what form of electricity your household appliances need to run & also whether it is an AC or DC supply that they require.

Store/Supply element:

The batteries – these store the electricity that has been harnessed by the system & stores it until the power is needed by the consumer. Here is a simplistic view of how these components all fit together:

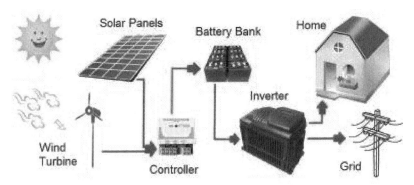

Figure 1 Simplistic view of the components (P Xavier © 2017)

Can this Power the world?

The simple answer is yes. Professor Mehran Moalem of Berkley University in the US has calculated that the total world energy usage in 2015 was 17.3 Terawatts of continuous power (this total was derived from the world totals for coal, oil, hydroelectric, nuclear & renewables, all converted into electrical watts).

This 17.3 Terawatts could theoretically be harvested using just 335km x 335km of solar panels. This would equate to an area of 43,000km^2. To put this in perspective, in Africa, the Sahara Desert covers 3.6 million km^2. Therefore, by placing solar panels over just 1.2% of the Sahara Desert, the world's energy needs could clearly be met[9]. Obviously, as people's power needs increase, so too will the amount of solar panels needed to meet the demand.

It is therefore feasible to harvest the sun's free energy to provide useable power to the world. As a result, it would be expedient to closely examine the components that you can utilise to provide electrical power to your own little part of the world.

But first, it will be a good idea to briefly explore & therefore understand electricity before looking at wind turbines in greater detail.

---

[9] https://www.forbes.com/sites/quora/2016/09/22/we-could-power-the-entire-world-by-harnessing-solar-energy-from-1-of-the-sahara/#3477e580d440 – 09/09/2017

Chapter 3 - Some notes on electricity

Before we start investigating the various components that are needed in any given system, it is worth quickly refreshing something that you no doubt studied in school. So this is a quick refresher.

Voltage is the measure of electrical potential. It is measured in volts (V). This can be thought of as pressure. If you think of water travelling through a pipe, the greater the pressure pushing the water through that pipe, the greater the volume of water will travel through that pipe every minute. If you now envisage a solar panel being connected to a battery, then the electricity will 'flow' to the battery. The greater the voltage being produced by the panel, the more electricity will flow into the battery.

If there is no voltage, then there is no current. There is no 'flow'. Nothing is moving. Power is only present when voltage & current are present.

Current (or amperage) is the measure of the flow of electricity. This is expressed as amperes or amps (A). This can be thought of as how fast something is moving; imagine a car travelling at 60mph on a motorway, then the electricity is travelling from the solar panel to the battery at 60 amps.
The speed at which electricity travels is actually very fast, much quicker than a car can travel. One amp is the equivalent to 6 billion, billion (6.2415×10^{18}) electrons per second. Therefore 60 amps is extremely fast.

Electrical **Resistance** is the value given for how much a conductor opposes the flow. It is expressed in Ohms (Ω). It is the relationship of voltage & current, therefore if low resistance is desired then you need a high voltage, not high current. Which is basically opting for a much bigger pipe to allow a larger flow of water, not pushing water very fast through a small straw. The small straw would offer resistance & therefore seem to fight back.

So that's what the basic terms mean, now for some school boy maths & it should be noted that you do not need to commit this fully to memory or even understand it. It is here so that you can refer to it at any point if you need to use it. After all, it may prove to be useful.

Ohm's law

Ohm's Law states that at a constant temperature, the electrical current that flows through a fixed linear resistance is directly proportional to the voltage applied across it & it is inversely proportional to the resistance. Therefore the relationship between the voltage, current & resistance is what Ohm's Law is based upon & it is always expressed in amps.

Ohm's Law is expressed mathematically in the following formula:

$$I = \frac{V}{R}$$

The values are as follows:

$$Current(I) = \frac{Voltage(V)}{Resistance(R)}$$

The following triangle will help aid the understanding of Ohm's law.

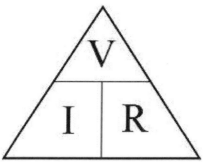

Figure 2 Ohm's law triangle (P Xavier © 2017)

Using the letters from this simple triangle will give each of the following formulae because the position of the individual letters relate to their position within Ohm's law triangle:

$$V = I \times R$$

$$I = \frac{V}{R}$$

$$R = \frac{V}{I}$$

So, by knowing any two of the values (current, voltage & resistance), the third can be calculated.

To find the voltage (V):

$$V = I \times R$$

Which is $V(\text{volts}) = I(\text{amps}) \times R(\Omega)$.

To find the current (I):

$$I = \frac{V}{R}$$

Which is $I(\text{amps}) = V(\text{volts}) \div R(\Omega)$.

To find the resistance (R):

$$R = \frac{V}{I}$$

Which is $R(\Omega) = V(volts) \div I(amps)$.

Now, to consider power (P). This is simply the rate at which energy is absorbed or produced within a circuit. Therefore a power source will deliver or produce whilst the connected load will absorb it. Consider a light bulb. This receives electrical power & converts it into light & heat energy. The higher the bulbs wattage, the more power it will receive & use. By simply following the same principles observed in Ohm's Law & substituting the values for electrical power, the following can also be calculated.

$$P = V \times I$$

The values are as follows:

$$Power(P) = Voltage(V) \times amps(I)$$

As seen previously, by knowing any two values it will be possible to calculate the power & the power triangle will help when remembering power calculations.

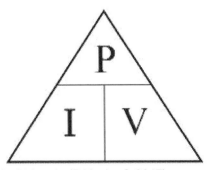

Figure 3 Ohm's law 2nd triangle (P Xavier © 2017)

As previously, using the letters in their position in the triangle will give the formula:

To find the power (P):

$$P = I \times V$$

Which is $power(watts) = vamps(I) \times volts(V)$.

Also,

$$P = \frac{V^2}{R}$$

Which is $power(watts) = V^2(volts^2) \div R(\Omega)$.

Also,

$$P = I^2 \times R$$

Which is $power(watts) = I^2(amps^2) \times R(\Omega)$.

Therefore it can be seen that a whole host of useful values can now be derived by just knowing two values. Here is a useful list of formulae which could prove to be useful when wishing to derive further electrical information:

To find the voltage from current & resistance:

$$V = I \times R$$

To find the power from current & resistance:

$$P = I^2 \times R$$

To find the resistance from voltage & current:

$$R = \frac{V}{I}$$

To find the power from voltage & current:

$$P = V \times I$$

To find the resistance from power & current:

$$R = \frac{P}{I^2}$$

To find the voltage from power & current:

$$V = \frac{P}{I}$$

To find the current from voltage & resistance:

$$I = \frac{V}{R}$$

To find the power from voltage & resistance:

$$P = \frac{V^2}{R}$$

To find the current from power & resistance:

$$I = \sqrt{\frac{P}{R}}$$

To find the voltage from power & resistance:

$$V = \sqrt{P \times R}$$

To find the resistance from voltage & power:

$$R = \frac{V^2}{P}$$

To find the current from voltage & power:

$$I = \frac{P}{V}$$

These twelve formulae should therefore be referenced if any of the values need to be calculated. Now it's time to examine the system components in detail.

Chapter 4 - Wind turbines

Wind turbines have been used for thousands of years. It has been estimated that the first type of wind turbine was used in Persia at some point between 500 – 900 AD & there are even records of a 'wind wheel' being used by Hero of Alexandria. You may even be familiar with more modern windmills in the UK which were used to grind grain into flour. Records indicate that these became established at some point in the 11th or 12th Century in the UK.

James Blyth created the first electricity generating wind turbine in Marykirk, Scotland in July 1887 & used it to charge a battery. In the UK, the first wind turbine that fed the National Power Grid was installed in the Orkney Islands in 1951.

So it can be seen that the technology has existed & been developed over hundreds of years, but since mankind adopted the use of fossil fuels, further development of wind turbines was relegated to a somewhat niche special interest topic & therefore the only developments were with micro-sized turbines. Things changed with the anti nuclear protests in the 1970's & since then, wind turbines started to see developments once more. This has now snowballed & the current political climate has now made wind turbines a viable source for energy production.

Where does wind come from?

All sources of energy on the planet originate from the sun. Wind is no exception. As the earth turns every day, the part that is facing the sun receives heat energy. The majority of the heat from the sun is received at the equator & it gradually reduces towards both poles.

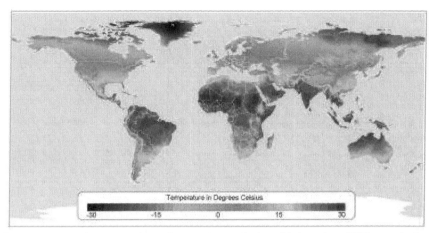

Figure 4 Annual average heat from solar radiation (University of Wisconsin © 2016)

The heated areas produce hot air & this is at a high pressure. Colder air is at a lower pressure. These temperature & pressure differences coupled with the Coriolis force (This deflects the direction of the wind to the right in the Northern hemisphere & to the left in the Southern hemisphere) create wind.

This is why the wind-flow around low & high pressure systems circulates in opposing directions in each hemisphere) & also the fact that the earth is a spinning sphere allows for the creation of very complex wind & weather patterns around the globe & gives the UK a prevailing South Western wind system. Figure 5 shows the average wind speed in the UK between 1981 & 2010.

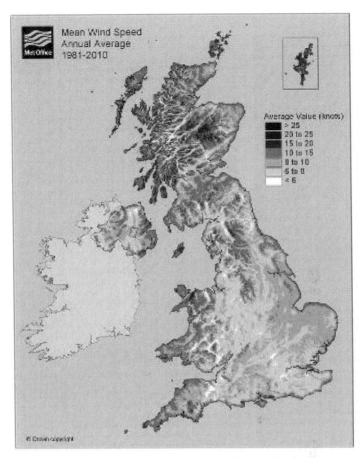

Figure 5 UK annual average wind speed (Met office © 2011)

The strongest wind recorded in the UK was at the summit of Cairngorm on 20th March 1986 & peaked at 173mph. Other strong winds were recorded at Fraserburgh, Aberdeenshire which had a wind speed of 142mph on 13th February 1989, Kilkeel, County Down which had a wind speed of 124mph on 12th January 1974 & also Gwennap Head, Cornwall which had a wind speed of 118mph on 15th December 1979.

Most of the maximum recorded wind gusts in the UK have occurred during the winter as winter is the windiest time of year in the UK. This is because the jet stream tends to move further South allowing more Atlantic storms to hit the UK.

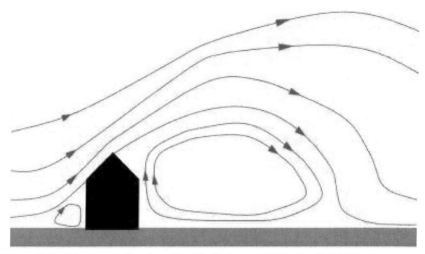
Figure 6 Buildings creating localised turbulence (P Xavier © 2017)

The local geography will also greatly affect the wind speed as mountains & hills will experience high wind speeds, but they will also shelter the valleys in-between. Also, buildings & trees will also have the same effect & act as buffers for the surrounding areas. Buildings can also cause areas of localised turbulence, where the wind is buffeted & re-circulates, as can be seen in figure 6.

There is however a rule of thumb, the higher the land, the greater the wind speed & the more open the land is, the greater the wind speeds. This can be seen on the map in figure 5, where hilly & mountainous areas are windy, whilst the valleys have a far lower average wind speed.

The wind speed scale

Wind speed at 10m		Beaufort scale	Description
m/s	knots		
0.0 – 0.4	0.0 – 0.9	0	Calm
0.4 – 1.8	0.9 – 3.5	1	
1.8 – 3.6	3.5 – 7.0	2	Light
3.6 – 5.8	7 – 11	3	
5.8 – 8.5	11 – 17	4	Moderate
8.5 – 11	17 – 22	5	Fresh
11 – 14	22 – 28	6	
14 – 17	28 – 34	7	Strong
17 – 21	34 – 41	8	
21 – 25	41 – 48	9	Gale
25 - 29	48 - 56	10	
29 - 34	56 – 65	11	Strong gale
>34	>65	12	Hurricane

Types of wind turbine

There are a huge amount of wind turbines available to purchase & there are also an infinite amount that have been created by DIY'ers. However, they all fall into two broad types. Horizontal axis wind turbines (HAWT) & Vertical axis wind turbines (VAWT). Both types have their advantages & disadvantages.

Horizontal axis wind turbines (HAWT)

The horizontal axis wind turbines are the type that most people think of when they think of a modern wind turbine. They are after all the most common type to be seen in UK on-shore wind farms, in the media & in UK off-shore wind farms. They can also be said to have a similar design to a windmill.

HAWT have the main rotor shaft & electrical generator placed at the top of a tower & they must be pointed into the wind. Small turbines are pointed by a simple wind vane placed square with the rotor (blades) or with a trailing vane, while large turbines generally use a wind sensor coupled with a servo motor to turn the turbine into the wind.

Most large wind turbines also have a gearbox, which turns the slow rotation of the rotor into a faster rotation that is more suitable to drive the electrical generator. Since a tower produces turbulent air behind it, the turbine is usually pointed upwind of the tower.

Figure 7 Horizontal axis wind turbine (Patrickmark © 2008)

Wind turbine blades are also made stiff to prevent the blades from being pushed into the tower by high winds. In addition, the blades are placed in front of the tower & are sometimes tilted up a small amount.

Downwind machines have been built, despite the problem of turbulence, because they do not need any additional mechanisms for keeping them in line with the wind.

Also, during times of high winds, the blades can be allowed to bend which reduces their swept area & therefore also reduces their wind resistance. Since turbulence leads to fatigue failures, & reliability is important, most HAWTs tend to be upwind machines.

HAWT advantages

HAWT can be placed on very tall tower bases that allow access to stronger winds in sites with wind shear. In some wind shear sites, every ten meters up the wind speed can increase by 20% & the power output increase by 34%. HAWT are a highly efficient design. As the blades always move perpendicularly to the wind, they receive power through the whole rotation. In contrast, all vertical axis wind turbines involve various types of reciprocating actions, requiring airfoil surfaces to backtrack against the wind for part of the cycle. Backtracking against the wind leads to an inherently lower efficiency in design.

HAWT disadvantages

HAWT require a large tower construction which is required to support the heavy blades, gearbox, & generator. Also, the heavy components (gearbox, rotor shaft & brake assembly) will need to be craned into position. HAWT are generally set at a great height & this makes them visible across large areas, disrupting the appearance of the landscape & sometimes creating local opposition.

Downwind variants suffer from fatigue & structural failure caused by turbulence when a blade passes through the tower's wind shadow (for this reason, the majority of HAWT use an upwind design, with the rotor facing the wind in front of the tower). HAWT also require an additional yaw control mechanism to turn the blades toward the wind. They also generally require a braking or yawing device in high winds to stop the turbine from spinning & destroying or damaging itself.

Anatomy of HAWT

All HAWT share the same common elements. They are shown in figure 8.

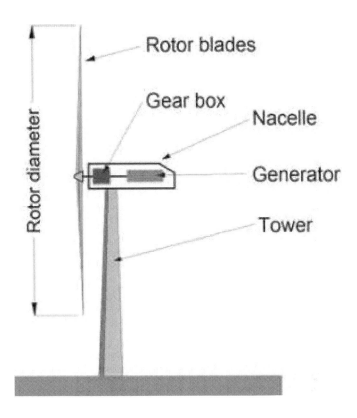

Figure 8 Anatomy of a horizontal axis wind turbine (P Xavier © 2017)

The rotor blades are all connected to the central hub, which turns through the gearbox & generator. Figure 9 shows a cutaway of the nacelle & its internal components.

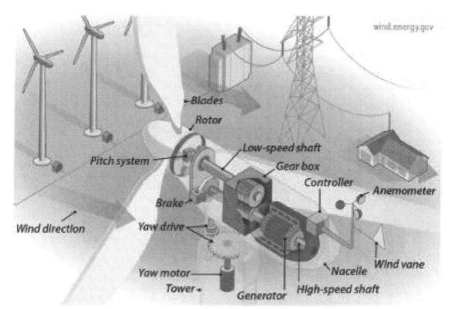

Figure 9 Cutaway of a HAWT nacelle & internal components (US Department of Energy © 2014)

These illustrations show the larger HAWT of the type that are used by the National Grid in the UK, Europe & North America, but any commercially available HAWT for domestic use will have mostly the same components but on a much smaller scale.

Vertical axis wind turbines (VAWT)

VAWT are different in that they have the main rotor shaft arranged vertically.

VAWT advantages

The main advantage of this is that the wind turbine itself does not need to be pointed into the wind. They therefore have the advantage on sites where the wind direction is highly variable or has turbulent winds.

On a VAWT, the generator & other primary components can be placed near or on the ground, so the tower does not need to support heavy equipment, this makes maintenance easier. Also, no yaw mechanisms are needed.

A VAWT has a lower wind start-up speed compared to a HAWT. A VAWT may be built in locations where taller structures are prohibited. A VAWT situated close to the ground can take advantage of locations where rooftops, mesas, hilltops or ridgelines funnel the wind & increase wind velocity.

VAWT disadvantages

The main drawback of a VAWT is that they generally create drag when rotating into the wind. It is also difficult to mount vertical-axis turbines on to towers, meaning they are often installed nearer to the base on which they rest, such as the ground or a building rooftop. The wind speed is slower at lower altitudes, so less wind energy is available for a given sized turbine. Air flow near the ground & other objects can also create turbulent flow, which can introduce issues such as vibration, including noise & bearing wear which may increase the maintenance or shorten the service life.

However, when a turbine is mounted on a rooftop, the building generally redirects wind over the roof & this can double the wind speed at the turbine. If the height of the rooftop mounted turbine tower is approximately 50% of the building height, this is near the optimum for maximum wind energy & minimum wind turbulence. Most VAWT have an average decreased efficiency compared to a HAWT, mainly because of the additional drag that they have, as their blades rotate into the wind. Versions that reduce drag produce more energy, especially those that funnel wind into a collector area.

Having rotors located close to the ground where wind speeds are lower do not take advantage of higher wind speeds at greater height. There are also various subtypes of the VAWT.

Darrieus wind turbine

The design of this type of turbine was first patented by the French aeronautical engineer Georges Jean Marie Darrieus in 1926 & still carries his name. Darrieus wind turbines are comically also called Eggbeater turbines, because they can look like a giant eggbeater. They have good efficiency, but produce a large torque ripple & cyclic stress on the tower, which contributes to poor reliability. Also, they generally require some external power source, or the addition of a Savonius rotor to start it turning because the starting torque is very low. The torque ripple is reduced by using three or more blades which results in a higher solidity for the rotor. Solidity is measured by blade area over the rotor area. There are however major difficulties in protecting the Darrieus turbine from extreme wind conditions & in making it self-starting.

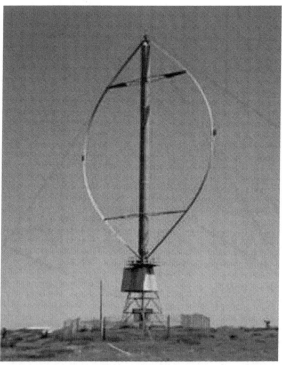

Figure 10 Darrieus wind turbine (Public Domain Image © 2007)

Newer Darrieus type turbines are not held up by guy-wires but have an external superstructure connected to the top bearing.

H-rotor gyromill wind turbine

When Darrieus patented his wind turbine he also made an inclusion for any vertical airfoils. Therefore a design of the Darrieus with vertical blades is now commonly known as H-Rotor Gyromills, despite being within Darrieus' original patent.

Figure 11 H-Rotor gyromill (Public Domain Image © 2016)

Helical Darrieus wind turbine

When the blades of a Darrieus wind turbine are twisted into a helix (3 blades & a helical twist of 60°), it is known as a Helical Darrieus. It is the best design in the Darrieus family as the wind pulls each blade around on both the windward & leeward sides of the turbine. This has the advantage of spreading the torque evenly over the entire revolution, therefore preventing any destructive pulsations.

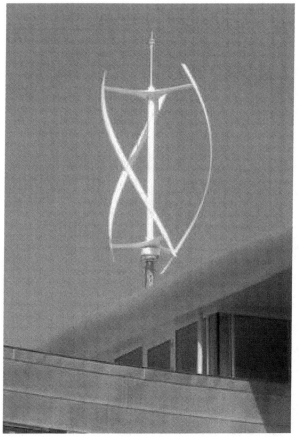

Figure 12 Helical Darrieus wind turbine (Anders Sandberg © 2007)

Anatomy of VAWT

All VAWT also share the same common elements. They are as follows:

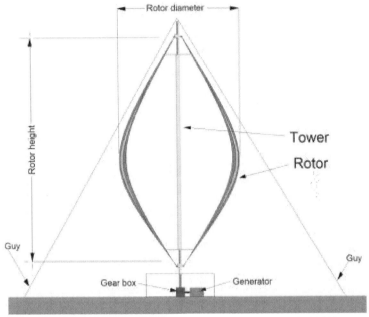

Figure 13 Anatomy of a vertical axis wind turbine (P Xavier © 2017)

How a turbine turns in the wind

If you have not seen a wind turbine or windmill spinning in the wind, you will at least be aware that they do spin in the wind. They do this because of the Bernoulli Effect. It is the same principle that allows aeroplanes to fly.

In an aeroplane's wing, the air flowing past the top surface of the wing is moving faster than the air flowing past the bottom surface. Bernoulli's principle states that the pressure on the surfaces of the wing will be lower on the top surface compared to the lower surface.

This pressure difference therefore results in an upward lifting force lifting the aeroplane up by the wings. The wings are shaped so as to cause the airflow around the top surface to travel a greater distance than the flow around the bottom surface. As can be seen in figure 14.

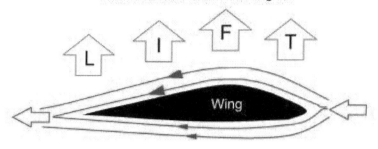

Figure 14 The Bernoulli effect (P Xavier © 2017)

This has the effect of an aircraft wing sucking itself & the aeroplane upwards, this is 'lift'. If you now envisage a three bladed propeller & each of those propeller blades have the same profile as the wing in figure 14, as the air passes over the blades, they will suck on one side (as the pressure is lower than the other side) thereby spinning the propeller. A wind turbine is the same as the propeller, except the wind is spinning the propeller.

The winds kinetic energy is being harnessed & transferred into electricity by the generator. Or, to put it another way, the kinetic energy of the wind is being turned into torque energy which turns the generator.

The amount of energy which the wind transfers to the rotor depends on the density of the air, the rotor area, & the wind speed.

Air density

The kinetic energy of a moving body is proportional to its mass (weight). The kinetic energy in the wind therefore depends on the density of the air. The kinetic energy of a moving body is proportional to its mass (or weight). The kinetic energy in the wind therefore depends on the density of the air. In average atmospheric pressure conditions at 15°C, air weighs 1.225 kg/m^3. However, the density decreases slightly with increasing humidity & it is also denser when it is cold rather than when it is warm. At higher altitudes, (in mountains) the air pressure is lower, & the air is less dense. The chart below shows the relationship between temperature & weight.

Density of air at standard atmospheric pressure

Temperature °C	Air density of dry air kg/m^3	Max. water content kg/m^3
-25	1423	-
-20	1395	-
-15	1368	-
-10	1342	-
-5	1317	-
0	1292	0005
5	1269	0007
10	1247	0009
15	1225	0013
20	1204	0017
25	1184	0023
30	1165	0030
35	1146	0039
40	1127	0051

Rotor area

The rotor area determines how much energy a wind turbine is able to harvest from the wind. As an example, if you imagine a 500 kW wind turbine having a rotor diameter of 25m (this is much bigger than you could install at a domestic property). This equates to a rotor area of some 625m^2.

Since the rotor area increases with the square of the rotor diameter, a turbine which is twice as large will receive 2^2 = 2 x 2 = four times as much energy. Therefore a turbine with a rotor diameter of 50m will have a rotor area of 2,500m^2.

Wind turbines deflect the wind

In the real world, all wind turbines deflect the wind to some degree before it reaches the rotor blades, therefore it will never be possible to harness 100% of the wind energy. In fact, the maximum that is possible to extract is always less than 59% (Betz' Law). Therefore only 59% of the kinetic energy in the wind can be converted to mechanical energy by using a wind turbine.

Also, it should be evident (as energy cannot be destroyed, it just moves from one form to another) that if 59% of the wind energy has been captured, then 41% has not, but has just passed through the rotor blades. The more kinetic energy a wind turbine pulls out of the wind, then the more the wind will be slowed down as it leaves the rear of the turbine. This does make sense if you consider that if you were able to extract all the energy from the wind, then no air would move away (after passing the rotor blades) it would have a speed of zero.

Therefore the air could not leave the turbine. In that case it would not be possible to extract any energy at all, since all of the air would obviously also be prevented from entering the rotor of the turbine.

In the other extreme, the wind would pass though your turbine blades without being slowed down at all. In this case the rotor blades would not have extracted any energy from the wind at all.

It is clear then that there must be some way of braking the wind which is in between these two extremes & is the most efficient way when converting the energy in the wind to useful mechanical energy. This is what is explained in Betz' Law.

Therefore the effect of deflection can best be seen as a bottle neck.

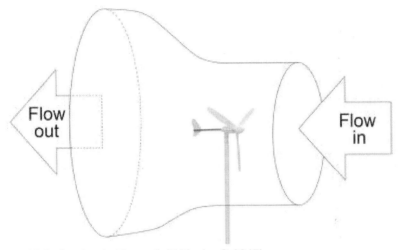

Figure 15 Deflection bottle neck (P Xavier © 2017)

The wind turbine rotor will slow down the wind as it captures the kinetic energy & converts it to rotational energy. Therefore the wind will be moving more slowly behind the rotor blades than in front of them (as a percentage of the wind energy is converted). As the amount of air entering through the rotor blade sweep area from the right (front (every second)) must be the same as the amount of air leaving the rotor area to the left (behind), the air will have to occupy a larger cross section (diameter) behind the rotor plane.

The bottle neck in figure 15 demonstrates how the slow moving wind on the rear (left hand side in the image) will occupy a larger volume behind the rotor blades. The wind will not be slowed down to its final speed immediately behind the rotor plane, the slowdown will happen gradually behind the rotor, until the speed becomes almost constant & equalises with the wind surrounding the bottle neck.

Air pressure distribution in front & behind the rotor blades

As wind approaches the rotor at the front, the air pressure gradually increases as the rotor blades act as a barrier to the wind. As it goes through the blades the pressure drops & then gradually increases to the ambient air pressure level. Figure 16 demonstrates exactly how this happens.

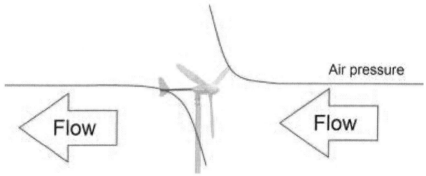

Figure 16 Air pressure distribution (P Xavier © 2017)

It should be clear from figure 16 that the air pressure will drop immediately behind the rotor plane (to the left). It then gradually increases to the ambient air pressure level in the area.

Further downstream the turbulence in the wind will cause the slow wind behind the rotor to mix with the faster moving wind from outside the bottle neck area, thereby equalising the wind speed & pressure. The affects on the wind will therefore gradually diminish the greater the distance from the rotor blades.

The power of wind

Wind speed is extremely important for the amount of energy a wind turbine can convert into electricity. The energy content of the wind varies with the cube (the third power) of the wind speed. If the wind speed is twice as fast, it contains eight times as much energy.

$$2^3 = 2 \times 2 \times 2$$

This is all because of Newton's second law of motion, which can be demonstrated with the following observation. If the speed of a car doubles, it will take four times as much energy to brake down to a complete stop.

In the case of a wind turbine, the turbine uses the energy from braking the wind & if the wind speed doubles, the rotor blades get twice as much wind moving them every second & that doubling contains four times as much energy (as was demonstrated in the car braking example).

The following formula for power per m^2 in Watts can be used to demonstrate this principle.

$$\text{Power} = 0.5 \times 1.225 \times v^3$$

This assumes that there is an air density of 1.225kg/m^3, with dry air at 15°C at sea level & v is the wind speed (cubed). The following chart can also be used.

m/s	W/m²	m/s	W/m²	m/s	W/m²
0	0	8	313.6	16	2508.8
1	0.6	9	446.5	17	3009.2
2	4.9	10	612.5	18	3572.1
3	16.5	11	815.2	19	4201.1
4	39.2	12	1058.4	20	4900.0
5	76.2	13	1345.7	21	5672.4
6	132.3	14	1680.7	22	6521.9
7	210.1	15	2067.2	23	7452.3

This however is only the theoretical power & in practice the value will be a lot less. A value known as the power coefficient (C_P) is the ratio of the actual power output compared to the theoretical available.

$$C_P = \frac{Actual\_Power}{Theoretical\_Power}$$

After analysing Betz Law, it is evident that the power coefficient (C_P) is unlikely to be greater than 0.593. It should therefore be evident that the wind speed has an important effect on the power output from a turbine. The power in the wind is proportional to the cube of the wind speed. (If the wind speed doubles, the power output increases by eight times).

The following chart shows the Betz Theory power output for a turbine using density as 1.225 kg/m3.

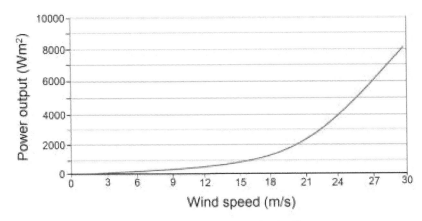

Figure 17 Betz Theory power output (P Xavier © 2017)

To calculate the power of the wind passing perpendicularly through a circular rotor area can be calculated with the following formula.

$$P = 0.5 \times \rho \times v^3 \times \pi \times r^2$$

ρ = The density of dry air (1.225) in kg/m^3.
v = The velocity of the wind in m/s (meters per second).
r = The radius of the rotor arms in meters.

However, placing a wind turbine on a rooftop will not yield the power results that you might desire.

Rooftop power

An example for power can be demonstrated if a 1kW turbine is installed on a rooftop, it might be expected to generate 1kW an hour & therefore 24kW per day (1kw x 24 hours).
However this would be an incorrect assumption. Firstly, this would only be true if the wind was blowing consistently at the rated speed for a full 24 hours. The turbine's rated speed is just a measure of how much power the turbine will generate at the highest wind speed that the turbine can tolerate.

Therefore it is its maximum output, not an average, a mean or median. The relationship between wind speed & power output can be seen in figure 18.

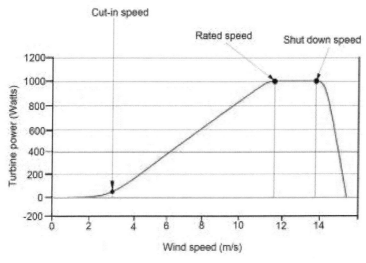

Figure 18 Speed & power output relationship (P Xavier © 2017)

As can be seen, the 1kW turbine starts to generate power at approximately 3m/s. This is the cut-in speed. If the wind is slower then it simply will not turn the rotor blades & therefore will not generate any electricity.

When the wind speed increases above the cut-in speed, then so too will the amount of electricity up to the turbine's rated output (which in this example is just under 12m/s. At this speed the turbine is pumping out 1kW (1,000w) of electricity. Not far above the rated speed is the shut down speed (just under 14m/s in this example). It is here that the turbine will start to turn on the brake to stop the turbine damaging itself.

This is always just a little over & above the rated speed. The rated speed can be thought of as the maximum spot where the turbine is maxed out & it will take no more speed & give no more electricity. It's basically all downhill after the rated speed.

As was stated earlier in the chapter, mountains, valley's, buildings, trees & all structures that are above the ground will all cause localised turbulence. They will also slow the surrounding wind speed, as can be seen in figure 19.

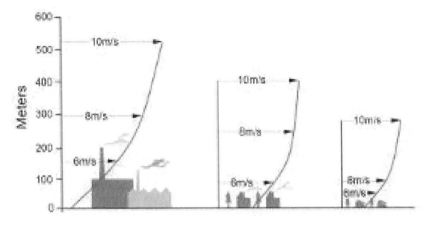

Figure 19 How ground structures effect wind speed (P Xavier © 2017)

This shows that the higher the obstacle, the lower the surrounding wind speed, therefore the higher the elevation needs to be to be in a faster wind flow. This is due to the roughness of the topography.

Orography

At a height of 1km, the air flow is hardly influenced by the earth's surface. Below this level, the friction caused by the features on the earth's surface affects the flow considerably. Wind based industries call how the wind is affected by the roughness of the earth 'the orography of the location'. As a rule of thumb, the more 'rough' (more obstacles to the wind) an area is, the more the wind will be slowed down. A large city will obviously have a huge effect on the wind flow, whilst an open area such as an airport runway will not. Long grass & shrubs will also slow the wind, whilst a flat open desert will not.

All types of landscapes have been given a 'roughness class' which acts as an aid when calculating the orography factor on a specific area. These are called 'roughness classes' or 'roughness lengths' (this is the theoretical distance above the ground where the wind speed should be zero). The roughest & highest end of the scale has lots of buildings & trees, whilst the flattest landscapes score the lowest.

The following table details each of these classifications.

Roughness class	Roughness length (m)	Energy index (%)	Landscape type
0	0.0002	100	Water surface
0.5	0.0024	73	Completely open terrain with a smooth surface such as a concrete runway in airports, mowed grass etc.
1	0.03	52	Open agricultural area without fences, hedgerows & very scattered buildings. Only softly rounded hills
1.5	0.055	45	Agricultural land with some houses & 8 metre tall sheltering hedgerows with a distance of approx. 1,250 metres
2	0.1	39	Agricultural land with some houses & 8 metre tall sheltering hedgerows with a distance of approx. 500 metres
2.5	0.2	31	Agricultural land with some houses & 8 metre tall sheltering hedgerows with a distance of approx. 250 metres
3	0.4	24	Villages, small towns, agricultural land with many or tall sheltering hedgerows, forests & rough or uneven terrain
3.5	0.8	18	Large cities with tall buildings
4	1.6	13	Very large cities with tall buildings & skyscrapers

There are numerous free calculators on the internet that will calculate the anticipated wind energy at a given location, however beware that the wind speeds that the DTI website provides have been shown to be far too ambitious. To obtain accurate data, it is imperative that real world readings should be used. Therefore actual wind speeds should be measured at your own site.

A convenient way to measure wind speed

The measurement of wind speed is usually done using an anemometer. There are two main types. A fixed type which uses cups on a frame that rotate in the wind, or the handheld turbine type. The cup type is usually fixed to a pole with the addition of a vane to also indicate the direction of the wind.

There are a few other anemometers, they include ultrasonic or laser anemometers which detect the phase shifting of sound or coherent light reflected from the air molecules. Hot wire anemometers detect the wind speed through minute temperature differences between wires placed in the wind & in the wind shade (the lee side). In practice, the fixed cup type is used in most scenarios.

Turbine noise

All wind turbines also produce noise to some degree. Listening to a hum or whirl from your own wind turbine may be a pleasant reminder to you as you will know that it is making you money or saving you money. However your neighbours may not be so keen to listen to it. As such, the noise that will be generated should be a consideration.

After all, the unhelpful bureaucrats at your local Planning Department will concern themselves if they suspect there could be a noise based issue, or if they receive any noise complaints.

To give you an idea on how noisy a small wind turbine can actually be, a well known 6kW wind turbine (suitable for domestic use) on the UK market produces 45 dBA at a wind speed of 5 metres per second & 65 dBA with a wind speed 20 metres per second.
To give you some concept on just how loud this is, consider the following data.

>	30dB – Whispering, leaves rustling very gently.
>	60dB – Normal conversation.
>	90dB – In the middle of city traffic.
>	120dB – Rock concert.
>	150dB – Jet engine at 10m.

Therefore if a turbine is set next to a busy road in a town or city then it would not be noticeable. If it was set in a small hamlet with no through traffic then it will be very noticeable, especially during a summer's evening/night when the neighbours have their windows open. Also, most people are tolerant of their own noises, but intolerant of other people's noise, so even a quiet whispering can be an issue for some people. Therefore anyone living within one mile of a wind farm can hear the farm & as such their property value will be reduced. However, no location is ever completely silent. All birds, animals & human activities will emit sound & at winds speeds around 4 - 7m/s & up, the noise from the wind on leaves, shrubs, trees etc. will mask any audible sound from a wind turbine.

There are two distinct types of noise sources within a wind turbine. The first is the mechanical noise produced by the gearbox, generator & other parts of the drive train. Secondly, there is the aerodynamic noise produced by the passage of the blades through the air.

Since the early 1990s there has been a significant reduction in the mechanical noise generated by wind turbines & it is now usually less than, or of a similar level to, the aerodynamic noise.

Aerodynamic noise from wind turbines is generally unobtrusive – it is broad-band in nature & in this respect is similar to, for example, the noise of wind in trees. However, a properly maintained & installed wind turbine should not cause too much of a noise problem.

In recent years, the turbine manufacturers have been busy reducing the noise emissions. They no longer use standard industrial gearboxes, but instead use purpose built gearboxes that have been adapted for wind turbine use & therefore are now much quieter. Also, turbine blades were also found to resonate & thereby emit noise. They are now designed not to resonate & thereby noise from this source has also been reduced. Similarly on some larger turbines there are purpose drilled holes drilled in the nacelle & chassis frame to minimise any noise resonating from those components. Finally, the nacelle & components are now shrouded in sound insulation. All of these small enhancements have helped greatly reduce noise emanating from wind turbines.

Now all turbines (from 1.5 – 50kW) that you can purchase will have noise data available from the manufacturer or vendor. It is imperative that you check the acoustics label or data before committing to any purchase. Using that data, any professional installer will be able to calculate the 'noise' that is expected to be experienced from the nearest window (including neighbouring properties as well as your own) that originates from the turbine's hub. The quieter the turbine, the closer to a property it can be located, so garden size & noise levels could prove to be a restriction to some potential turbines.

Calculating the sound level expected from the turbine

The sound level decreases by approximately 6 dB(A) (10*log 10^2) every time the distance doubles from the sound source. The next table assumes that any sound reflection & absorption will cancel each other out.

$$\text{The surface of a sphere} = 4\pi r^2$$

r = The radius of the sphere.

If the sound emitted from the turbine has a power of (x) W/m^2 hitting a sphere with a certain radius, then it will have the same power hitting four times as large an area, if the radius doubles.

Alternatively, it can be simplified by examining the next table.

Distance (m)	Sound level change dB(A)	Distance (m)	Sound level change dB(A)
9	-30	100	-52
16	-35	112	-53
28	-40	126	-54
40	-43	141	-55
50	-45	159	-56
56	-46	178	-57
63	-47	200	-58
71	-49	224	-59
80	-50	251	-60
89	-51	282	-61

The table should be used as follows. If the wind turbine has a noise level of 50dB(A), then at a distance of 9m it will be 20dB(A) & at 28m it will be 10dB(A).

Flicker

Wind turbines also create what is known at the flicker effect. That is the shadow that the wind turbine creates when it is rotating. This can be very much like a strobe light & therefore the shadow that is cast over the year (position of the sun on its zenith, sunlight's intensity, time of year) must be considered so that the flickering shadow is not cast on any windows. Your local authority will obviously insist that your expensive wind turbine is removed if a neighbour has epilepsy & the strobe like flickering from the turbine causes them to have epileptic fits.

Choosing a mount

There are a few options to consider when selecting how & where to mount a turbine. That is, will it be a roof mounted turbine or freestanding (pole or mast) mounted. Domestic sized wind turbines come in a range of sizes, prices & power ratings that can generate anything from less than 100W to around 50kW. Small micro-turbines are also available & can be used to charge batteries, but turbines of 600W upwards are a more suitable size to generate electricity for your home &/or business. It may even allow you to power an electric vehicle if you cover a modest mileage. Therefore the actual size of the mount & position of your mount will be dependant on the size of the wind turbine. The size of the turbine is dependant on your output requirements. To calculate which size will best fit your requirements, please see chapter 7. If you are thinking that a roof mounted turbine would best suit your needs, then it would only suit your needs if you want a visible statement to your neighbours stating that you have green credentials. In almost every scenario they perform extremely poorly.

In fact most individuals who have installed turbines on their roofs have regretted their actions. This is all due to the fact that any turbine placed near a roof ridge will receive only weak, turbulent winds. Several field trials have found that building mounted turbines perform poorly; producing only a small fraction of the energy they would produce if sited on open ground, on a tower above & away from any buildings. Also, turbines can & will resonate in the wind & produce vibrations in the building. In addition, forces acting on the turbine during high winds can damage the building structure. All of which was explained earlier in this chapter.

All building mounted turbines are therefore useless for harnessing a useable amount of energy from the wind. This is partly because they are physically connected to the building structure & top heavy. As such they are only suitable for the smallest turbines which are typically rated between 400w – 1kW.

Therefore there are lots of people voicing their concerns about their roof mounted installations. One such complainant gives this example. His installation has only generated 20p worth of electricity over several months (following installation). That system would therefore take 1,800 years to cover the installation costs. A roof mounted turbine will never be in an air zone that will give a sustained speed & as the wind around a building is turbulent, the turbine will spend more time chasing the wind (as the wind will be fluctuating erratically) rather than harnessing it. A roof mounted turbine is therefore not a realistic option. It should therefore be clear that it would be sensible to install a freestanding tower if there is a suitable location on your property. Also, to have a power & cost effective turbine, it will need to be sited in a location where there will be strong & sustained winds.

There are two main types; freestanding & guyed. There are also considerable differences in the tower & installation costs between the two, as well as the amount of space the different styles can take up. Freestanding towers are like flagpoles as they have no extra support other than their concrete bases.

They can either be a monopole (tubular) type or lattice type (similar to the Eiffel Tower). The problem with freestanding towers is that the wind will always be pushing against them & therefore the action of the wind will always be trying to push the tower over, therefore all freestanding towers require sizeable concrete foundations to support them. They do however have the advantage of having no guy wires.

Guyed towers

Guyed towers require much less foundations as their surface area is greater. They require al least three sets of guy wires & three sets of guy wire anchors.

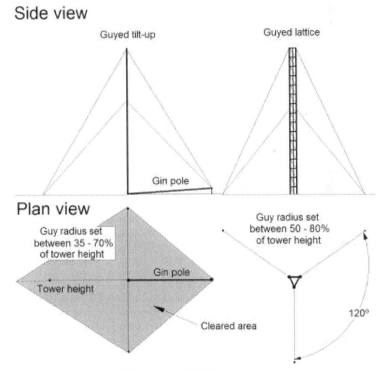

Figure 20 Guyed towers (P Xavier © 2017)

On all types of tower, it is important to construct them as high as possible to harness as much of the wind as possible (within legal limits).

Tilt up towers are clearly the most practical. The reason for this statement is that no-one will ever need to climb to the top & maintenance can therefore be undertaken at ground level. They are relatively cheap & can be constructed by a competent DIY'er. They can also be raised & lowered in less than an hour. They require four sets of guy wires.

Three are set into concrete anchors placed at separate points around the tower's on the radius. The fourth set is attached to the gin pole which gets attached to the fourth concrete anchor when the tower is raised. The shaded grey area in figure 20, at the base of the tower is the area that will need to be cleared of any trees, shrubs & structures so as to allow the guy wires to lie down cleanly when the tower is resting on the ground. Also, there needs to be a further area cleared to allow a vehicle to pull the tower upright, or a permanent or semi-permanent winch constructed to raise & lower the tower if there is not a suitable vehicle to use. The downside of a tilt-up is that it is possible to accidentally drop the tower if any vehicle winching the tower were to skid or slip. If the guy anchors are not positioned correctly then they too could snap.

Another type of guyed tower is a fixed tower. Once the tower has been constructed, it is not designed to be lowered back to the ground. Again it can be a monopole or lattice. However, a monopole may prove difficult for maintenance as a ladder will need to be used to access the top, whilst a lattice can be climbed when maintaining the turbine at the top. Both types need to be craned into position due to the heights involved & great care must be taken at the construction stage as craning is dangerous. Any accidents during the build phase can be hazardous to health. The guy wires are best set at 120° so as to form a triangular formation radiating from the tower & set into three sets of guy wire anchors set into reinforced concrete pads in a radius around the perimeter of the tower, so as to counteract the wind shear forces.

The radius of these pads should be between 50 – 80% of the height of the tower & be amply sized to resist the wind force pulling them out of the ground. The construction costs can be similar to the tilt up type, but has the advantage of using less ground space as it will never need to be lowered to the ground. The range of lattice towers are fairly wide as many radio hams use these towers to affix their aerials. Therefore there are many on the market & it is therefore even possible to buy a second-hand tower of this type on internet auction sites & in the classified sections of various radio ham magazines.

Freestanding towers

Freestanding towers are far more expensive when compared to guyed towers, but they have the advantage of having no guy wires, do not tilt over & use only the smallest footprint area to be installed.

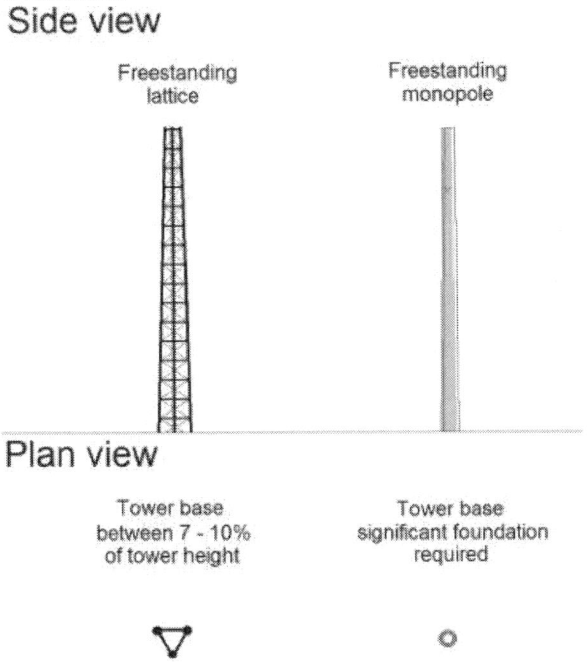

Side view

Freestanding lattice

Freestanding monopole

Plan view

Tower base between 7 - 10% of tower height

Tower base significant foundation required

Figure 21 Freestanding towers (P Xavier © 2017)

There are the three of four legged freestanding lattice (Eiffel tower) type & the monopole type. The lattice towers are generally constructed with tubes & angle irons which are welded together. The monopole types are made from sections of tubular steel which taper towards the top.

Both types of tower will require a crane to lift the various sections into position, as well as the turbine. This adds both time & cost as well as adding potential danger to the installation. The lattice towers can however be climbed when maintenance is required, but the monopole type can be somewhat difficult when maintenance is required. Any free standing tower can cost at least 33 – 50% more than a guyed tower.

The aesthetics of the freestanding towers are far better for most individuals as there are no guy wires.

Tower selection

When you have selected which turbine best fits your needs, then the data issued by the turbine manufacturer will inform you as to what size tower will be required to house it. You can therefore work backwards either selecting which type you wish to use.

It may be a case where you wish to design & build your own guyed tilt up or guyed lattice tower. In that case the data provided by the turbine manufacturer will be enough to allow you to calculate what size tubing &/or angle iron you will need to construct your tower.

If your site is very small, then this may force you to adopt a freestanding lattice or freestanding monopole. If the site is not level or has obstructions, then the guyed tilt up can be excluded. If your site does not allow for deep reinforced concrete foundations, then a guyed tower will be your only option. Your own site & requirements will reveal which is best for your needs & your site's needs.

Personal power, National Grid or both?

Another choice that will need to be made is if your turbine will be used solely for providing power to your batteries, will it also be tied in to the National Grid, or will you opt to benefit from both.

All three options are permissible, but if you opt for one over the other then you will be missing out on something. For instance, if you solely use the turbine to charge your batteries, then you will never benefit from receiving money from your energy supplier for the electricity that you produce. If you solely export the electricity to the National Grid, then you will be selling electricity at a low cost & buying it back at a higher cost, without utilising what you have produced yourself.

The third option, to do both will (for most people) be the best option. That is using the electricity you have produced for your own needs, then when your batteries are full, exporting the surplus electricity to the National Grid for which you will be paid.

Both the first options seem to be somewhat short-sighted & therefore by utilising the third option you can have the best of both worlds, but please examine chapter 11 for the relevant legislation before committing to this option for your own exacting electricity needs.

Fulminology

The study of lightning (Fulminology) has revealed that the earth is hit by lightning around the globe approximately 40 – 50 times every second. This amounts to 1.4 billion strikes every year. However, 70% of these strikes are centred on the tropics. Figure 22 shows the annual frequency of strikes per km^2.

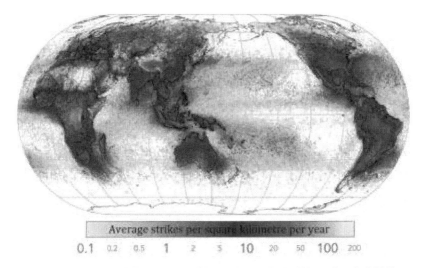

Figure 22 Global annual frequency of lightning strikes (Citynoise © 2008)

This does not mean that the UK, Europe or any other place that is not situated within the tropics can be considered immune to lightning strikes. The UK annually has 300,000 lightning strikes & approximately 30% of those are estimated to cause some level of damage. Therefore protection from the possibility of a lightning strike would be prudent as lightning can deliver 300,000 amperes (30kA) in a split second (Lightning travels 90,000 mi/sec). A large bolt can even deliver 120kA. It would therefore be a wise move to plan against the possibility of these currents destroying your PV/turbine system.

Such a system will not prevent a lightning strike occurring, but will reroute the lightning's electrical energy away from a PV/turbine installation's delicate components & through a predetermined lightning friendly route, thereby minimising the chances of fire & damage to the installation. It will not give 100% protection, but will significantly reduce the risk.

Lightning will always look for the quickest route to the earth, therefore anything that stands above the earth will be a target as it is higher than ground level. Therefore any wind turbine &/or ground mounted PV panel will be an obvious target for lightning.

Protection for PV system

The process of installing lightning protection involves grounding all the racking installed for the PV panels & the electrical wiring system. This will have the effect of discharging all the accumulated static electricity & reduce the possibility of a lightning strike. The fuses & breakers installed in the system will not act fast enough to provide protection from a lightning strike, therefore all the electrically conductive parts of the installation will need to be bonded & all the electrical cabling need to share a path to ground & that is achieved with a grounding rod[10].

Part of any lightning protection will also involve surge arrestors & surge capacitors. These absorb electrical surges from the lightning strike but do not act independently; they still need to be properly linked to the grounding rod. An arrestor clamps onto electrical wiring & in the event of a lightning strike, the surge from the lightning will prefer to travel through the connector to the ground as the distance will be shorter. A capacitor will operate in a similar way but will act faster than an arrestor.

If your PV system is situated away from a building, then the likelihood of damage will be greatly increased. Also, the electrical cabling can act as a conduit for the surge. It would therefore be desirable to install an arrestor next to the PV panels &/or turbine. Also one to protect the charge controller, one on each side of the inverter (DC & AC side) & also one next to a generator if you have one. All these should be seen as countermeasures to protect your installation.

---

[10] BS 6651 states that a combined earth rod length of a system should be no less than 9m whilst each individual earth rod should be no less than 1.5m in length.

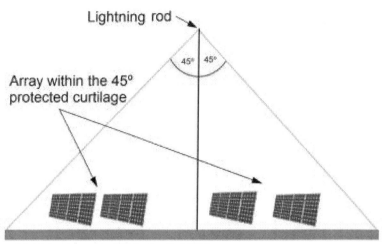

Figure 23 Lightning pole (P Xavier © 2017)

Another method of protection that can be employed would be an above ground lightning pole (like a flag pole without the flag). The pole will give protection to the surrounding area (45° from the tip) & act like an umbrella, shielding everything within its curtilage, as can be seen in figure 23.

It works because lightning will always try to find the quickest route to earth. If a lightning fork comes near the pole, it will use that as a conduit to earth rather than anything else as it will be the most direct route to earth. Also, if you opt to install a lightning protection system for your PV/turbine system, great care must be taken so that it will not interfere with any existing protection systems that may be installed at your property. If there is an existing protection system, a new system could interfere with the original lightning protected zone.

As a consequence, great care should be taken to make sure that the original protected zone is extended rather than disrupted. If this is not carefully considered, it could disrupt the original zone & therefore provide a path for lightning currents to enter the building, damage property & possibly endanger life.

Section 5 of the Electricity at Work Act 1989 states that all lightning conductors & earth grounding installations should be visually inspected & tested at regularly fixed intervals, preferably not exceeding 12 months. Whether your PV is a commercial enterprise or installed on private property for your own personal benefit, a bi-annual inspection regime would be the safest approach. Once in the spring following the winter storms & once again in the autumn before the winter storms start. These bi-annual inspections should be seen as a minimum as it would be beneficial to also allow for periodic inspections.

Also, if it is at all possible, all jointing in any earthing system should be bonded with exothermic welds wherever possible. A method that may be helpful would be to weld a section of copper-clad ground rod to the rebar (in reinforced concrete) & use this to connect the rebar to your grounding wires, again using exothermic welds.

Protection for the wind turbine system

Due to their exposed location & height, wind turbines are vulnerable to the effects of direct lightning strikes. As a consequence, a direct strike will cause significant damage to the components, structure & even catastrophic failure if adequate lightning protection has not been installed. An insurance company will not generally pay for lightning strikes on wind turbines as they classify them as 'an act of God'. Lightning protection should therefore be seen as an essential element to your wind turbine installation.

By using a combination of proper grounding, wiring, lightning & surge arrestors you can minimise the risk of lightning damage to any wind turbine.

Protection against lightning consists of three major areas. Each of which need to be correctly designed & installed for it to be in any way effective.

- Grounding the tower & equipment.

- Correct routing, shielding, grouping of cabling & equipment.

- Lightning & surge protection.

Grounding the tower & equipment

Perimeter ground

A single ground earth is not going to be of use when grounding wind turbines. Therefore the most effective earth is known as a 'perimeter ground'. The clue is in the name as it fully encloses the perimeter of the wind turbine & offers multiple, spaced out grounds, as can be seen in figure 24, where the circular base & the radials are the grounding cables. All these & the attached grounding rods are all set underground. The radials allow the electricity to travel away from the tower & dissipate into the ground.

If space is constricted at your location, then even a partial installation will be better than omitting the perimeter ground completely. For instance it is possible to install a truncated design, two or three quadrants etc., or whatever works best at your location.

Also, any grounding system that you adopt will work best in wet or water logged soil. If you have particularly dry soil conditions you could upgrade your subsoil by digging out the natural & replacing it with **bentonite** which is a type of moisture retaining clay.

This will therefore improve the grounding effect that you are trying to achieve. In addition, when mixing concrete for the foundations, it is possible to use **marconite** instead of sand because marconite is a granulated electrically conductive aggregate which will greatly increase the conductivity of the finished reinforced concrete.

Figure 24 Perimeter ground (P Xavier © 2017)

However, the downside of these two enhancements are that they are somewhat specialist items & therefore unlikely to be available at your local builders merchant.

Ufer ground
Another type of earth is known as an Ufer ground. This is basically a block of reinforced concrete set into the ground. Concrete is porous & therefore allows quantities of water to permeate through the concrete & thereby allow the concrete to make an effective ground for the purposes of lightning protection. It may be the case that you will be using reinforced concrete to support the base of your wind turbine, if this is the case, design the base to be larger than normal & it will then be possible to use the base as a ground.

Just remember to leave some rebar protruding from the top of the block to connect the grounding rods to. Better still, leave a section of the block unmade (rebar in place, but no concrete, to allow you to connect the copper grounding to the rebar inside the extremities of the block, then concrete over the connection so that it is completely enclosed within the concrete block so as to prevent galvanic corrosion (it has to be solid wire though, stranded wire will wick moisture into the concrete causing it to crack when it freezes).

Wherever possible, cast the concrete block directly into the bare earth without using any formwork. This will allow for the maximum surface area underground & therefore offer the maximum lightning protection. A point to remember is that it is underground, therefore it can be as messy as you like & nobody will know.

Tower to ground connection
It is not advisable to run a copper lightning conductor directly on a steel tower. Steel is not as conductive as copper, but it is conductive. Also, copper will dissolve any zinc coating that is present on the steel therefore it will just rust. It is therefore permissible to use the steel framing of the tower itself to act as a lightning conductor.

Any tower will also need guy wires to help support it during lateral loads (wind). These too will act as conduits for lightning. Each of the guy's will need to be grounded & physically attached to the ground; therefore once again reinforced concrete should be used. The guy's will need to be anchored into the ground, so the same earthing connection described in the Ufer section would be ideal. Again, do not connect anything copper to anything galvanised.

Also, to complete the system, run a cable through & connected to each of the reinforced concrete pads so that they are all interlinked & will therefore act in unison. This can take the form of a perimeter ground, but as before, it does not need to be perfectly circular as it will be underground & out of sight.

Also, as previously, all ground rods & connections should be underground & connected with exothermic welds wherever possible.

All three of the options discussed here rely on installation taking place in trenches & then being back filled. Whichever option or combination you adopt will no doubt be determined by the fiscal cost & site conditions as aesthetics would not be a consideration.

Cabling the tower & equipment

Any cables that come down the tower should either be in metallic conduit (EMT), or if you have a tubular-type tower they should run inside the tube. The reason for this is the **skin-effect**. That is energy obtained from a lightning strike will naturally want to travel on the outside of any the metal conduit. This will help keep that energy away from the cables because any metal conduit will form a **Faraday cage**.

The current involved in a lightning strike & the inductance of the tower can quite easily set up an instantaneous voltage difference between the tower top & bottom of 100 kV (100,000 Volts).

That means every foot of a 100 feet tower can have a potential difference of 1 kV, & by having the turbine power wires exiting the tower at 3 feet above ground level will just create a potential 3 kV voltage difference between those wires & the ground. That can be completely avoided by routing the turbine wires all the way down to the ground & then into the ground. Then, from there to their destination.

Even if there is a turbine disconnect near the tower, it is advisable to run the wires underground to a separate pedestal that houses the disconnect, then from there back again underground onward to the batteries.

Running the turbine wires underground to the inverter or charge controller will greatly help to lower any lightning strike energy travelling down those wires.

However, it is not going to prevent lightning from dissipating completely. The large amount of energy (often in the lower frequencies of the electromagnetic field) present in lightning can penetrate quite deeply into the ground. Any wires running in that ground will act as a transformer, coupling in to that energy.

That is how a nearby lightning strike can also couple into well-pump wiring & destroy the pump, pressure switches, & quite possibly also all the electronics hooked up to the house grid. A surge arrestor will therefore have to deal with that energy further down the line to protect the remainder of the system. If you site your turbine some distance from your house, the distance will create high impedance (resistance) in the cables & this will therefore help minimise the lightning strike from travelling down the cabling to your home & expensive electronics. If however you house the electronics at the base of the tower then there is little you can do to protect the delicate electronics from being destroyed by a lightning strike.

Lightning destroys electronics & electrical systems by creating voltage differences between the various wires & cables. These voltage differences can be huge & modern electronics are not designed to handle anything above their design rating. Therefore, the single point ground resolves this problem.

Single point ground
A single point ground is when all the cabling is routed to a ground bus. The cables enter on one side then exit on the other side. All the different ground connections, such as the house or grid ground, wind turbine ground etc. all connect to this ground bus. This would also be the location where the surge arrestors would be located to keep the voltages of all other cables (turbine phase wires, grid wires etc.) tied closely to the ground voltage.

The surge arrestors literally straddle the ground bar, making protected & unprotected sides on the ground bar. The equipment itself is only grounded through a single connection to the ground bus on the protected side. It is installed in a way that insulates it from other conductors (for instance the concrete floor as concrete is a conductor).

The result of a single-point ground is that the voltage of the equipment, including the equipment ground, can float up & down, even if it is thousands of volts.
As long as there is no voltage difference between the various wires of the equipment, or the equipment parts (such as an inverter or charge controller), there will not be enough voltage or large equalisation currents to cause any damage to the electronics.

Most scenarios now have to contend with an existing setup where the house is grounded on one side & the wind turbine cables comes in on the other side. The inverter should be located somewhere between them. There will also be other equipment such as household electronics to consider. This makes it impossible to follow the single point ground principle strictly. However, it is often possible to create multiple single-point grounds on a local scale & also include surge arrestors to provide a good level of surge & lightning protection.

Any of the above lightning protection enhancements you decide to use will only be 90% effective. There will always be a percentage of the lightning strike that will try to travel along your cables & try to fry your carefully designed home energy system. This is why lightning arrestors should also be included, regardless of whichever system you adopt.

Lightning arrestors

Lightning arrestors work by shorting excess voltage from a power carrying conductor to ground. This diverts the surge energy to ground, instead of going through any sensitive electronics.

There are roughly three types of lightning arrestors: The first type employs some type of spark gap. These are usually enclosed by a capsule & some type of gas which is sealed within it so it has predictable properties. These devices are often called gas discharge tubes, or GDTs. The good thing about a GDT is that it can handle very large currents. The most expensive can handle a direct lightning strike without any problems. However, they are relatively slow to respond, allowing a relatively large voltage surge to pass through them before they kick in & short the surge.

That voltage is generally larger than electronics can handle. The second type of arrestor uses a metal oxide that becomes conductive in the presence of a strong electrical field. These metal oxide varistors (MOVs) act as a resistor that conducts more electricity as the current though it increases. The let-through voltage of an MOV is much lower than that of a GDT & it is much more predictable, but their current handling capacity is much smaller & the let-through voltage can still get quite large for some strikes.

Another bad property of MOVs is that they tend to fail after a number of high-current conduction cycles & when they fail they do so as a short circuit. That means they should be fused in some way to avoid overheating or overloading of the circuit that they are protecting. The third type of arrestor involves semi-conductors such as zener diodes. They have the lowest let-through voltage & the best controlled clamping behaviour of the various arrestor types. Their weak point is that their current handling capabilities are the smallest of all.

Lightning arrestors are rated through various parameters.

The important ones are their rated voltage (the normal operating voltage for the device, where it does not affect normal operation), their nominal discharge current (the normal current they can handle repeatedly when clamping a surge), their let-through voltage (the maximum voltage left over by the device when it is clamping, usually at their nominal discharge current) & their response time (how long it takes for the arrestor to respond to a surge). The let-through voltage is sometimes described as 'clamp voltage' or 'residual voltage'.

Therefore it should be clear that there is no single ideal lightning arrestor device. That means a combination of devices & methods need to be employed to provide effective lighting protection.

Because of this, numerous lightning arrestors should be placed throughout your system. For a typical wind turbine install this means there should be a lightning arrestor close to the wind turbine alternator to protect the alternator & to take as much energy as possible off the turbine cables before they go to the inverter or charge controller (or batteries). Another should be placed directly before the electronics (rectifier, inverter, charge controller &/or batteries). Both sides of these items need protection too. It would also be recommended to also fit protection to any other electrical input sources into your home. Telephone, internet, cable TV, National Grid electricity etc., & it is important to remember a golden rule with lightning arrestors: keep the cabling as short & straight as possible. If you are using multiple wires tie them together.

A note on EMP's

Lightning does not have to hit your wind turbine or PV setup directly as a nearby lightning strike can cause what is known as an **electromagnetic pulse** (EMP) that will travel down electrical cables & that will also destroy your electronics.

An EMP can also be caused by the sun during a coronal mass ejection. This is known as a solar EMP & is created when a burst of plasma is ejected from the sun towards the earth, where it interacts with the Earth's magnetic fields & subsequently knocks out satellites & the Earth's electricity networks.

The biggest ever recorded was on 1st & 2nd September 1859 & is known as the Carrington Event. At this time the Northern Lights were visible from the North Pole to as far South as Sub-Saharan Africa. Telegraph systems across Europe & North America completely failed during this event. It gave the telegraph operators electric shocks & telegraph pylons sparked wildly. A similar sized plasma burst narrowly missed the Earth on July 23rd 2012, but still knocked out the electrical grid in Quebec, Canada. If another Carrington sized event ever had a direct hit on the earth, all the electrical, communications & computer networks would be destroyed within a split second. A properly protected system may therefore be the best insurance policy for survival after such an event.

Interestingly, an EMP is also produced by every nuclear explosion, therefore if a nuclear explosion were to happen in your vicinity, your home energy system will be protected.
Consequently, if you & your home energy system both live through a nuclear blast, you will have the means to power your electric TV & radio & be able to listen to the ensuing government propaganda broadcasts informing you that 'help is on the way'.

Chapter 5 - Cable management

The electrical cabling joining the system components together can be thought of as being similar to blood veins in the human body. Instead of being the conduit for blood in a human body, they allow for the flow of electricity to the essential system elements in the installation. Therefore, it is important that the cables are protected from damage.

Over time, the electrical cables will be subject to damage. This could be from mechanical damage from movement when the cables rub against something, such as if a cable is allowed to move in the wind & is continually rubbing against a wall or a frame. Cables can be damaged from the elements, such as the continual heat cycle when exposed to the sun & also UV damage from sunlight too. Insects, birds & vermin can also attack cabling, stripping the insulation. Cables can also be damaged by vandalism & even accidentally damaged. It is therefore imperative to protect the cables as much as possible.

There are therefore several methods available that can be employed to do this. Firstly, it is important that the cabling you employ is trimmed to the correct length for the job at hand. Too much will allow the cabling to physically move & therefore trimming to length will mitigate this problem. Whichever system you decide to use, it is important that you always trim the cables to the correct length.

Secondly, it is advisable to secure any loose cabling. This can be achieved by using cable ties of one sort or another, however these will all degrade when exposed to the sun's UV light, therefore these will need to be replaced periodically, or alternatively it is possible to use a galvanised fixing band which will not degrade in sunlight.

A better & more permanent solution would be use a conduit to house the cables. The first option would therefore be to use PVC trunking which can be easily cut to size to securely house the cables. Junction boxes & conduit boxes should be used to join various runs together & there are also numerous elbows & junctions available to help ensure the cable runs are completely sealed safely (without sharp turns) within the trunking, however this is more suitable for internal cable runs as PVC degrades in sunlight & PVC trunking can be eaten by rodents.

A more robust system would be to use galvanised metal conduit externally. This system is completely robust & can withstand the rigours of the UK weather. You however may need to purchase a suitably sized tap & die set to make a suitably sized thread on the end of the channels if you have cut them to size, also any cuts that are made need to be treated as the metal will be exposed on the cut ends. Any scratches that are made to the components during installation would also need to be treated to inhibit any chance of corrosion.

Any buried cable runs should be made with armoured cables so as to protect from any potential gardening/landscaping damage. It would also be advantageous to back fill any trenches with sand & to place electrical warning tape on top of the sand before backfilling the trench.

The cabling on the installation can last many years & the installation will not operate without it. Therefore whichever method you adopt to house the cables will be money well spent as you should never need to replace the cables if you adopt the correct method to protect the cables, cable runs & joints. Ensure that all cables are well protected from all hazards.

Back up power

There may be occasions when there is not enough sun, or not enough wind to adequately charge your batteries. A generator will therefore fill any shortfalls in any deficit suffered by your PV &/or wind turbine system, & therefore keep the lights on.

Hospitals & other large buildings have diesel generators that are designed to cut in when there are power cuts. You can use the same concept for your system, but on a much smaller scale. The cost need not be excessive for a small domestic generator & many can be purchased for just a few hundred pounds. There are numerous sizes with various levels of output available. Figure 25 shows one small inexpensive Chinese generator with a generic design that is currently on the market.

Figure 25 Inexpensive Chinese generator (Public Domain Image © 2017)

These generators are always listed online with their designed output level. Therefore you could opt for a 1Kw model, 3Kw, 5Kw etc.. The bigger the output, the greater the price. Also, these units are not designed to be permanently left outside, but it is unsafe to leave them working indoors, therefore, it may be prudent to house the generator in a small shed.

Also, as all internal combustion engines need clean air to function & need to expel spent air through the exhaust, it would be sensible therefore to create a fireproof exhaust that exits outside the shed & a fireproof air intake to feed the generator. These generators also generate a lot of noise, even the quieter ones. They are after all small motorbike engines. It would therefore be sensible to soundproof the small shed to minimise the noise level for yourself & your neighbours. Vibrations can also be a problem, so it would be beneficial to create a rubber mount to sit the generator on.

Whatever soundproofing & vibration proofing you use will benefit both you & your neighbours. Running costs are set to rise for petrol & diesel, but that is controlled by global demand & out of your control. One thing is certain, if you suffer from a few days with only a little sunshine & very little wind, then you may be glad that you installed a generator to top up the power to your batteries. Also, it will wait until it is needed, so you can plug it in as & when it's needed, then turn it off again when it is not needed. However, a word of warning, never fully charge your batteries from the generator as whichever batteries you purchase will be designed to be charged by the PV or the wind turbine & if you want the generator to kick-in automatically when the batteries drop below a certain level, then you will need to include an automatic transfer switch (ATS) & an automatic starter. These will start the generator when specific programmed conditions exist & switch the generator on, or off.

Your inverter & generator will also need to be compatible, as the inverter & ATS will need to be speaking the same language for it to operate as you intend.

Also, in 1900 Rudulf Diesel invented the diesel engine to run off peanut oil, so if diesel is in short supply (such as after 2040 when the UK & EEC intends to ban sales of petrol & diesel vehicles), then with little or no modification, the diesel generator could be run off waste cooking oil &/or renewable bio oils.

The main problem with waste cooking oil (WVO) is that it often contains cooking waste & water. It therefore needs to be filtered to clean the oil. WVO also has a different viscosity to regular diesel (RDO) & biodiesel (BDO); therefore the diesel engine/generator will not run with this oil straight after filtration. Biodiesel will run without modification because it has already been chemically treated to make its viscosity the same as regular diesel. Straight vegetable oil (SVO) also needs to be treated to make it the same viscosity as RDO.

To make filtered WVO & SVO the same viscosity as RDO, it needs to be heated to achieve the desired level of viscosity which is the same viscosity as RDO. Most individuals who run generators & vehicles from WVO & SVO use the same method. They have two tanks, one for WVO/SVO with a heating element & another for RDO. When the WVO/SVO reaches the desired viscosity, they switch from the RDO tank to the WVO/SVO tank.

Alternatively, the WVO & SVO can be treated by a process called transesterification, a fairly simple process that uses lye to remove the coagulating properties from the oils. The by product of biodiesel processing is just glycerine, which is used in soaps & other harmless products. Therefore this process will need to be undertaken before the oil is placed in the fuel tank. Most people who use this method undertake the entire process it in their garage or outbuilding.

The viscosity problem is caused because the majority of diesel engines/generators use an injector pump to feed the fuel into the engine. Older diesel generators used a positive displacement fuel pump which supplied fuel continuously to the injectors; therefore the viscosity of the fuel was never a problem.

If new generators were to be manufactured with positive displacement fuel pumps, then it would be possible to run clean WVO, RDO, SVO & BDO without any modification to the oils, or needing to pre heat it.

This would make clean efficient fuel a reality to everyone. In the USA, 'Affordable Power' has seen this gap in the market & has manufactured such a generator. It is called the 2-71 Detroit Diesel. This generator will run without any modifications.

Currently, many restaurants & café's are happy for people to remove their WVO either for free or for a small charge as they have to pay for someone to remove it. Therefore there is a clean free (or low cost) energy source that can be utilised to generate you electricity that you can use or sell to the National Grid. Also, this fuel source is carbon neutral (as it does not emit any more carbon than it absorbed when it was growing as a plant), The exhaust emissions are cleaner than RDO, it is made from renewable sources, WVO can be obtained locally to you as there will be restaurants & café's near to you & it will stop the potential of the oil from going into landfill.

Currently this source of energy is untaxed; therefore the government is keeping quiet about it rather than promoting it as a clean energy source. There may however come a point when the government decides to tax it. Until they do, it makes excellent fiscal sense to utilise it. If you do make suitable fuel, it would be easy to take the next step & convert a diesel powered car to run off WVO, SVO & BDO, rather than RDO.

Chapter 6 - Legislation in the UK

Planning permission

Domestic stand alone wind turbines

In England, provided all the limits & conditions listed below are met, the installation, alteration or replacement of a stand alone (not building mounted) wind turbine within the boundaries of a house or block of flats (provided there are no commercial premises in the block) can be considered to be permitted development & therefore do not need an application for planning permission.

- The project is permitted only if the stand alone wind turbine installation complies with the Microgeneration Certification Scheme Planning Standard (MCS 020)[11] or equivalent standards.

- The installation must not be sited on safeguarded land. Safeguarded land is defined as land which is necessary to be safeguarded for aviation or defence purposes & has been notified as such to the Secretary of State. It is possible to check & self certify online[12].

---

[11] http://www.microgenerationcertification.org/admin/documents/MCS%20020%20Planning%20Standards%20Issue%201.0.pdf – 20/09/2017

[12] http://aviationtool.communities.gov.uk/ - 20/09/2017

- In Conservation Areas, development would not be permitted if the wind turbine would be installed so that it is nearer to any highway which bounds the curtilage (garden or grounds) of the house or block of flats than the part of the house or block of flats which is nearest to that highway.

- Only the first installation of any wind turbine would be permitted development & only if there is no existing air source heat pump at the property. Any additional wind turbines or air source heat pumps at the same property require an application for planning permission.

- The highest part of the stand alone wind turbine must not exceed 11.1m.

- The distance between ground level & the lowest part of any wind turbine blade must not be less than 5m.

- An installation is not permitted if any part of the stand alone wind turbine (including blades) would be in a position which is less than a distance equivalent to the overall height of the turbine (including blades) plus 10 per cent of its height when measured from any point along the property boundary.

- The swept area of any stand alone wind turbine blade must be no more than $3.8m^2$.

- Permitted development rights do not apply to a turbine within the curtilage of a Listed Building or within a site designated as a Scheduled Monument or in national parks, the Broads, Areas of Outstanding Natural Beauty or World Heritage Sites other than Conservation Areas.

In addition to the above points, the following must apply to the turbine.

- Use only non-reflective materials on blades.

- The turbine must be removed as soon as reasonably practicable when no longer needed for microgeneration.

- The turbine must be sited, so far as is practicable, to minimise its effect on the external appearance of the building & its effect on the amenity of the area.

Building mounted wind turbines

Provided all the limits & conditions listed below are met, the installation, alteration or replacement of a building mounted wind turbine on detached houses (not blocks of flats) & other detached buildings within the boundaries of a house or block of flats (provided there are no commercial premises in the block) can be considered to be permitted development & therefore not needing an application for planning permission.

The parameters are the same as for a stand alone turbine, except:

- No part (including blades) of the building mounted wind turbine should protrude more than three metres above the highest part of the roof (excluding the chimney) or exceed an overall height (including building, hub & blade) of 15m, whichever is the least.

- No part of the building mounted wind turbine (including blades) must be within 5m of any boundary.

- The swept area of any building mounted wind turbine blade must be no more than 3.8m^2.

David Cameron (the ex PM of the UK) famously installed a wind turbine on his house, only to be forced to remove it a few days later by his Local Authority's Planning Department. It would therefore be sensible to comply with the planners whims.

Scotland, Wales & Northern Ireland

In Scotland, a building mounted development requires planning permission, but a standalone development does not, unless it contravenes the following:

- It is the only wind turbine at the property.

- It is situated less than 100m from your neighbour.

- It sits on a world heritage site; is on scientific research land; near a listed building or is near land for outlined for archaeological purposes.

In Wales, planning permission will be mandatory, regardless to which type of wind turbine is proposed.
In Northern Ireland, planning permission will be mandatory, regardless to which type of wind turbine is proposed. The planners are supposed to concern themselves with the visual impact, noise, impact on local heritage & ecology of the project.

The Building Regulations – Wind turbines

Any wind turbine installation in the UK will require Building Regulation approval, just as any PV installation would, but the criteria that building control would be interested in would differ.

Stand alone wind turbines

The following list should form a basis upon which to build upon when applying for Building Regulations approval.

Part A – Size weight & forces exerted through fixings. Certification of proposed materials.

Part B - Fire risk on PV installation due to possible over loading &/or short circuiting. Certification of proposed materials.

Part E – Sound generated by the turbines & certification of proposed materials.

Part K - Method of safe installation of all components when positioned at a height. Method of safe access & egress for maintenance of installation components. Correct selection, construction & use of access equipment such as scaffolding.

Part L - A wind turbine installation is recognised in many applications as a way of conserving fuel & power, because it involves generating energy in an environmentally-friendly way, rather than consuming it from the fossil fuel grid supplies.

Part M - Accessibility & placement of equipment to ensure easy access to inverters, monitors, fuse boxes, isolators etc..

Part P - Use of the correct size & position of cabling & connections. Bonding & earthing of components. Protection from damage by the ingress of water & dust, animal damage & also damage from humans from either an accidental source or vandalism. Methods to isolate system components. Correct selection & use of protective devices such as RCDs, fuses & isolators Labelling & warning signage. Certification of proposed materials. Part P is also applicable to anything in or attached to a dwelling, therefore a shed in a garden will apply, as will an outhouse or outbuilding, even greenhouses. It is even applicable to the land that is attached to a building. It is also applicable to any DIY work.

Building mounted wind turbines

Building mounted systems would be the same as stand alone system, except with regard to Part A, as building control will be interested in how the weight & forces exerted through fixings apply to the building fabric.

British Standards

There are many British Standards (BS) & International Standards (ISO) that UK Legislation refers to. One of these relates to 'Cable ratings & Locations'.

BS7671:2008 & Amendment 3 (2015)

The IET have produced a handy guide to BS7671:2008 & Amendment 3 2015. It covers cable sizes & they are placed together & grouped into tables concerning where they can go & which current they can carry. The mixture of these two things is called a Method & there are 7 methods. Their titles are:

- **Method A** - Enclosed in conduit in an insulated wall.

- **Method B** - Enclosed in conduit or trunking on a wall.

- **Method C** - Clipped direct.

- **Method 100** - In contact with plasterboard, ceiling or joists, covered by thermal insulation not exceeding 100mm.

- **Method 101** - In contact with plasterboard, ceiling or joists, covered by thermal insulation exceeding 100mm.

- **Method 102** - In a stud wall with thermal insulation with cable touching the wall.

- **Method 103** - Surrounded by thermal insulation including in a stud wall with thermal insulation with cable not touching the wall.

There are numerous other BS & ISO's that are applicable to solar energy systems. As such there are far too many to list within this book. If further information is required, then an internet search with the topic (such as photovoltaic panels) & the words 'British Standards', or 'International Standards Organisation' will forward you in the right direction. If however you do wish to read them in full, you may have to pay.

Further reading on legislation

The following documents may be worth researching if further information is required on planning or building regulations.

The Town & Country Planning (General Permitted Development) (Amendment) (England) Order 2012[13]. The Town & Country Planning (General Permitted Development) (Amendment) (England) Order 2008[14]. 'Planning Policy Guidance 2 (PPG2): Green Belts' was superseded by the National Planning Policy Framework[15].

'Planning Policy Statement 7 (PPS7): Sustainable Development in Rural Areas. By Design: Urban Design in the planning system, towards better practice' was also superseded by the National Planning Policy Framework[16], as was 'Planning Policy Statement 22 (PPS22): Renewable Energy'[17] & 'Planning practice guidance for renewable & low carbon energy (July 2013)[18]'.

---

[13] http://www.legislation.gov.uk/uksi/2012/748/contents/made - 20/09/2017

[14] http://www.legislation.gov.uk/uksi/2008/2362/made - 20/09/2017

[15] https://www.gov.uk/government/collections/planning-practice-guidance - 20/09/2017

[16] https://www.gov.uk/government/collections/planning-practice-guidance - 20/09/2017

[17] https://www.gov.uk/government/collections/planning-practice-guidance - 20/09/2017

[18] https://www.gov.uk/government/collections/planning-practice-guidance - 20/09/2017

Chapter 7 - The system design

Before you can design your system, you will need to understand what uses electricity in your home & exactly how much it uses. This is because if you design a small system but you actually need a much larger system, the system simply will not be able to cope with the demands you place upon it.

It is therefore essential that each & every item of electrical equipment in your home is looked at to determine just how power hungry it actually is. To make an accurate measurement use a plug in a kill-a-watt power meter. They are available to purchase online & typically range in price between £10 - £20 (see chapter 10 for more information).

These meters will inform you on the exact wattage for whichever appliance you are testing. You can then double check your readings with the designed wattage which should be evident on the appliance nameplate which you often find on the rear (or bottom) of the appliance.

Also, if you are replacing any electrical items, it would be advisable to replace them with more energy efficient models, thereby lowering the overall running cost & the ultimate load on your system.

For instance, it will be cheaper to install & use energy efficient lighting at your property rather than install a PV/wind turbine system to power inefficient lighting. The same is true for all appliances that you plan to use at your property.

Calculating your load

Consider this. If there are 10 incandescent light bulbs in your home where 3 are rated at 100w & 7 are rated at 60w then this is a total of 720w. If these are replaced with their equivalent in energy efficient bulbs, then that would equate to 3 at 55w & 7 at 30w, which is a total of 375w, so there is a huge saving already, but if the incandescent lighting was replaced by LED lighting, this would equate to 3 at 20w & 7 at 7w which works out to 109w.

Therefore there is an instant saving just by switching light bulbs. It is more cost effective to do this than pay several thousand pounds to build an energy system to provide power to the lighting; therefore the most cost effective system is the smallest system that will meet your needs.

However, lighting is not the only thing in your home that use electricity, therefore a detailed study will have to be made so that you know exactly what is using electricity & just how much. This may sound like a simple task, but also consider that it is highly unlikely every electrical appliance in your home will be in operation at the same time.

If for instance you look at a kitchen, chances are that the light will be on in the evening, as well as the cooker & hob. The fridge & freezer will be on 24/7, but smaller appliances such as a mixer or food processor will only be used for a short duration & probably not at the same time as the oven, but perhaps a radio may be on whilst someone is cooking in the kitchen. However, for the purpose of this example, it will be assumed that each of these electrical appliances are all switched on at the same time.

If it is assumed that there are 3 energy efficient bulbs which are equivalent to 60w bulbs, that would equate to 3 x 30w (90w). The fan oven can be assumed to be 2780w (but not running at full power, so assume 1700w) & an electric hob which is burning two rings at 7400w (two rings would be 3700w), a fridge at 1480w & a freezer at 1840w. A food processor may be rated at 750w & a mixer at 250w then the radio at 7w. If it is assumed that each & every one of these are all on for one hour (to make the example easier), the total would be:

90 + 1700 + 3700 + 1480 + 1840 + 750 + 250 + 7
= 9817w or 9.8kW

This example is over one hour so it is 9.8kW/h

This is a lot of electricity for one room over one hour. Also, another factor to consider is many appliances (the ones with electric motors such as hairdryers, food mixers, electric drills, circular saws etc.) may be rated at a particular wattage, but that is how much electricity is needed to keep them running. To get them started & to get them up to speed they could require twice or three times their 'rated power consumption', therefore this 'in-rush current' will need to be measured. To do this, you will need a clamp meter or multimeter that has a surge function (see chapter 10 for more information). Until you know what the actual power need is for that particular electrical appliance, you will never be able to accurately predict the needed electricity supply.

There is another point to be aware of. Your electrical items will also use a percentage of their 'rated power' when they are on standby. You no doubt knew that already, but did you know exactly how much this actually costs in electrical energy? Some items can use 90% of their rated power, some 80%, some 75% etc., some can use a lot less, perhaps 5%. As an example, if you consider a 100w television using 50% on standby, it will be using 50w when it is standby mode.

If the television is switched on & used for 6 hours a day, that would be 600w used, now add the standby time for the remainder of the day 18 hours at 50w is 900w. Add them together (900w + 600w) to get the daily electrical demand for the television (1500w aka 1.5kW). Standby power can potentially consume a lot of power & this is notoriously difficult to estimate accurately. The best method is to use a kill-a-watt power meter to measure exactly how much power the appliance is using when it is in standby (see chapter 10 for more information on the kill-a-watt meter). The next step is to create an inventory for your entire house, working out the exact wattage each item requires (remember that the wattage should be listed on the rear or base of every appliance or even in the manual. If you cannot find it, check online).

If you have a kill-a-watt power meter, it would be advantageous to use that to note the 'in-rush current' for all the appliances that have motors. Do not forget to include your hot water pump, even if you have gas central heating, the pump will be an electric pump. Also, decide what is necessary in your home. Perhaps there is a hair dryer (or some other item) that nobody uses. This is an ideal time to sell it, bin it or take it to the charity shop.

After all this, you should see that the list you have created is very long. The advice here is to now decide what is vitally important, what is not. For instance, there may be two mobile phones in the house, these would no doubt be very important items for their users & they would not wish to be without them. These would therefore be important items & should be prioritised. If you have Christmas tree lights, these would be very low priority compared to the mobile phones. Given a choice, who would rank their Christmas tree lights over their phone? Those lights are therefore consigned to being of no importance.

The next step is to take the time & see just how long each of the important items are being used for every day or every week. You will therefore be able to accurately work out your annual energy use & demands.

After working through your inventory, you should now have the wattage for every item in your house, know exactly how long they are used for every month & have labelled each of them all as being either priority items or non priority items. This is where you will be making two charts which will enable you to compare how much energy is currently being used, with a realistic minimum figure that you could use.

The following chart is a reduced list as it contains only items that are considered important & is being used here as an example. However, your list should ideally follow the same format, but only contain items that are deemed important by you.

Appliance	Wattage (w)	Use (hours)	Daily use (Wh)	Important
TV	160	6	960	Yes
Lights	6 x 60	6	2,160	Yes
Oven	1,700	1	1,700	Yes
Kettle	1,500	1	1,500	Yes
Fridge	1,480	24	1,480	Yes
Freezer	1.840	24	1,840	Yes
Phone	10	8	80	Yes
Radio	7	2	14	Yes
Hi-Fi	60	2	120	Yes
Total			**9,854**	

From this list, it should be obvious that just running the electrical items that are important, would still require almost 10kW/h, therefore that would be the minimum size system that would be required to meet the needs for the above list. It is also advantageous to include some spare capacity in case another appliance is purchased & added to the list.

However, a system to meet a modest need of 10kW/h will never operate at 100%, therefore a 15kW, or better still a 20kW system should allow for any unfavourable weather, system inefficiencies & if there is a surplus of electricity at the end of each day, it could be sold off to the National Grid to make a little money.

System costs

A home energy system that would meet these modest needs will never be cheap. It will require a considerable investment. If you have calculated your important list of items, then you will now know what size system you need.

In the UK, the cost of a 6kW wind turbine system (if you opted to have an installer construct the system) would be in the region of £20,000, but a smaller system would cost less.

4kW - £5,500	5kW - £6,500	6kW - £7,500

A roof mounted 1kW system would cost in the region of £3,000 (if you opted to have an installer construct the system). As has been seen previously, roof turbines are not efficient & therefore a larger tower mounted system would be more suitable, but would cost considerably more.

2.5kW - £10,000	6kW - £20,000	10kW - £30,000

As was seen previously, to be eligible for payment under the governmental FIT's, you will need to buy suitable systems from an MCS approved contractor to be instantly eligible for payments. A DIY system will have to receive certification & then apply through the Roo-FIT scheme.

Obviously if you constructed your own wind turbine energy system yourself as a DIY build, you would make considerable savings (you could half the costs listed in this chapter), but if you want a system that has a guarantee & warranty which is instantly eligible for FIT's payments, then you will be forced to use an MCS approved contractor & a MCS approved system. However, the choice is down to the individual.

Payback

For the example system listed here, it could cost £30,000 as has been seen earlier, but just how long would it take to recuperate this sizeable investment? That is a very difficult question to answer as there are so many variables & every system is unique. Also, energy costs fluctuate & the cost of the system components are set to fall. Everyone's usage levels are different, the FIT's tariff fluctuates due to governmental initiatives & the general cost of energy is set to rise considerably in coming years.

Therefore it is only possible to give a general idea, but it will always be changing as the variables always change & so do the targets. You should therefore recalculate your findings annually if you wish to have a reasonably accurate set of figures.

You should know how much you pay for your electricity (if not, it is printed on your electricity bill) & if you followed the exercise earlier in this chapter you should know how much electricity your household appliances are using. You can therefore see how much your energy expenditure is costing you every day.

Any system you install will never be 100% efficient & therefore a prediction on the expected output is impossible, but after you have installed any system, you can deduct what you've generated from what you would've bought from your energy supplier. That will be a cost saving every month. Also, if you are eligible for the FIT's payments, you can include that too.

The savings you have made to your energy bills will add up & eventually there will be a point in time when these payments will have covered the cost of your energy system & then will be making money as the savings & income will be pure profit.

Therefore you are the only person who can accurately calculate your potential savings. However, here are some payback periods for typical systems to consider.
If a wind turbine is sited in a very good position, it could take 21 years to start making a profit.

The payback period is completely generalised, but as the cost of electricity is only going to get more expensive & at the same time the demand will also increase, the likelihood of power cuts are now looming large on the horizon. Therefore, the payback periods will clearly reduce in coming years (due to the increasing cost of electricity) but you will also have the added benefit of being able to keep the lights on during these impending power cuts.

Chapter 8 - Maintenance

Maintenance will always be ongoing & will need to be carefully programmed into your diary. It is not something that should be skimped on, or omitted from your schedule. It will need to be taken seriously & it will be advisable to keep an ongoing record of each of the elements & if possible also to keep photographs so as to compare the condition of the system elements with how they were perhaps a year ago. No matter how good you think your memory is, it will not be good enough to remember the exact condition of something the previous year. It may also be helpful to communicate any problems you find via email to the manufacturer or installer so you can attach photographs of a component that is degrading year on year.

Each element of the installation will need to be examined in turn & it may be helpful to develop & set a routine. Also it is best to keep a close eye on the systems so that you are familiar with how they perform during various weather conditions. Then, you will be instantly alerted to any problems if they occur. Providing you rectify a problem in good time, your energy harvest should only have a minimal period of down-time.

Wind turbine maintenance

Wind turbines have a design life of between 15 & 20 years & typically can have a warranty period between 2 & 10 years, but there will be certain requirements that you will need to undertake for the warranty to be effective & therefore keeping a detailed diary (with photographs) will help prove you have inspected the installation & the condition of the elements.

You should also adhere to any/all of the recommendations in the warranty paperwork to ensure you are fully protected. If you have an installer to fit the system, then they should leave you with a maintenance checklist to follow. As a 6kW wind turbine installation can cost in the region of £27,000 - £30,000, it is an expensive element to any home energy system, as such it is imperative that the maintenance schedule should be followed regularly & to the letter, or it could prove to be an expensive folly.

If you consider that the blades of a wind turbine can travel as many miles in four months as a car can do after several years (100,000 miles), then the maintenance is extremely low, but it is very important as a poorly maintained wind turbine is liable to destroy itself. Therefore the turbine should be thoroughly checked twice a year as a minimum & also after any heavy storms.

Binoculars may be beneficial to help you examine the turbine if you are standing at ground level. However, if you see any potential defects, you will need to erect a scaffold tower or securely fix a ladder to closely examine the turbine.
Most modern wind turbines are not designed to have serviceable parts, but if you use an old machine found on an internet auction site, it may well need bushes or bearings that need to be replaced periodically.

The inspection of the turbine should be undertaken when considering the turbine as a whole, rather than concentrating on various individual components, but the nature of the wind turbine spinning & oscillating in the wind will loosen bolts (also turnbuckles on guyed towers) & damage the hardware, therefore it will be important to tighten all the bolts & fixings from time to time.

If you are going to climb a tower or lower a tilt-up tower, then first check the foundations for any anchor movement.

This may be an indication of a failed or failing foundation system. Also look for any deterioration to the anchor rods or other attachment points, especially where they contact concrete or the ground.

Examine the towers overall appearance. Check that it is straight & plumb. Small discrepancies are acceptable; however an out-of-plumb tower can be an indication to a more significant problem. At the very least, it could be dangerous to climb or tilt. Also check it for rust, since deep-rooted rust will affect the towers structural integrity.

Minor surface rust is to be expected, but not a huge amount. Probe any rusty areas with a small screwdriver or bradawl. Also, check for any broken welds or structural components that are bent out of shape or completely missing. Bent or missing tower parts may be easy to spot, but cracked welds are not. Rust streaking around galvanized welded joints may be an indication of a cracked weld. If there is any rust present on the tower, wire-brush rusty areas & apply a cold-galvanizing spray or paint. If a safety-climb system such as a ladder-safe system is installed, check the cable & tensioner integrity. Fall-arrest systems should not be used for support at any time until the entire fall arrest assembly is thoroughly checked.

With guyed towers, inspect all hardware: turnbuckles, equalizer plates (which equalize the tension on each set of guy wires), cable clamps etc., for any signs of deterioration, excessive movement or uneven tightness. Look for loose or missing lock nuts & turnbuckle safety loops. If these are missing they can cause a tower to collapse. Check all the guy wires for any rust & broken or frayed strands.

Pay close attention to the area where the cable passes around the thimble at the guy ends. This is a high-stress area & therefore subject to vibration, corrosion & these areas can often be difficult to see. Minor surface rust or the occasional missing guy cable strand may not present a major issue at present, but will need watching. Once corrosion starts, it can accelerate very quickly, especially if your site is near to the coast as it is subjected to salt-air environments. Some tower grounding conductors are connected directly to the guy wires. Galvanic reaction from dissimilar metals may cause corrosion inside the attaching hardware, therefore remove, inspect & replace anything that is suspect.

Check the guy tension is correct & adjust as needed. This varies between tower manufacturers, so follow the proper procedure for your tower. The tangential intercept method (using a bit of geometry & the sag of the cable) is often used for tilt-up towers; the oscillation method (using some math & a controlled shaking of the cable) is routinely used for fixed guyed lattice towers. Your wind turbine installation manual may inform you which method to use for your tower.

With a freestanding tower, inspect the hardware that secures the tower to the foundation. Look for any signs of unusual movement around the hardware & the leg flanges, such as misalignment, weathering patterns, or damaged bolts. If grout was used under the tower legs, check the drain-holes for any blockages & clean as necessary. Any moisture build up inside hollow tower legs can lead to freeze damage then a premature collapse of the tower. Never climb an ungrounded tower. First, look for proper grounding of the tower & any guy wires. Again, examine the manual for your tower. Inspect the grounding wire & the associated hardware. The most common problems found are loose &/or missing ground-rod clamps.

With regard to the brake, inspect & test the tower mounted turbine disconnect & shorting brake. If it is applicable also check the furling or brake mechanism for proper operation. (This should not be undertaken in a high wind). Brake, short, or otherwise secure the turbine before ascending the tower. Look for any signs of damage on all & any conduit, cable runs, junction boxes & conduit fittings for signs of water intrusion, condensation, animal/insect attack, cracks & frost-heave. Also, be aware that long conduit runs that were improperly installed can contain rather a lot of water, so be aware of this fact when you open any junction boxes.

Check cable terminals on all the components (disconnects, junction boxes, inverter, controller) for proper tightness & any sign of electrical arcing or any other signs of degradation. Test all the fuses & circuit breakers for electrical deterioration using the continuity tester on a multimeter & also be aware of any physical deterioration. Cartridge fuses can deteriorate over time, especially when used in outdoor locations. Use a multimeter to check all surge arrestors & a megohmmeter on cable runs to check for ground faults. Skinned or cracked cable insulation in underground conduit is one of the most common causes of ground faults. At the very least, system performance will suffer. Some older inverters can be damaged by ground faults & if the equipment grounding system becomes compromised an electrical shock hazard can be present.

When the turbine is spinning in the wind, check for a balanced three-phase output. Allow for the fact that there will be variations in the wind speed & therefore the voltage while you are moving the probes of the multimeter. The main thing to check will be variations of 10% or more between each of the phases. It is advisable to perform this test two or three times to rule out variations caused by the changing wind speed. Perform any other turbine-specific electrical tests as recommended by the manufacturer's literature. The manual should also include the testing protocols for the turbine electronics.

For grid-tied inverters, test for the ability to disconnect when the grid goes down by turning off the inverter breaker & verifying that there is no voltage at the inverter output. After turning the grid breaker on, verify the 5-minute delay before the inverter reconnects to the grid.

For battery-charging controllers confirm that the charging set point programming is appropriate for your batteries. Also, verify the controller's ability to perform this function by checking with a multimeter to ensure the power is diverted when the high battery voltage set point has been reached. When applicable, test the electrical integrity & operation of the turbine diversion loads. Clean out the dust & debris from any cooling fans & vents. Heat dissipation is essential for the proper operation of electronic equipment & this also has a direct effect on the equipment's life expectancy. Over the entire tower & turbine, look for missing rusty or loose bolts, nuts, & locking nuts.

Figure 26 Rusting tie down bolts at tower base (Rust Bullet © 2017)

It would be good idea to keep several sizes & types of spare hardware to hand so you can inspect & repair or replace any missing items during the inspection. If applicable check for proper torque.

The tower manual should have the manufacturer's recommended torque specifications & bolt specifications, therefore you can include the appropriate sockets spanners in your tool box. While the majority of tower hardware can be tightened with a torque wrench that goes up to 340 Newton meters, but some tower hardware may require 475 Newton meters or even higher.

Inspect any or all tower-mounted data equipment, such as the boom, anemometer & wind vane. Also check cabling. The anemometer is an item that has moving parts & may therefore need to be replaced periodically.

The turbine is designed to be spinning, therefore is subject to mechanical wear & tear. Therefore any issues with the bearings could be difficult to spot, so learning to read your wind turbine can inform you about any sign of imminent bearing failure. This could be rust streaks, as this can be caused by moisture entering then exiting the bearing, which usually leaves a very distinctive, rust-coloured residue. This is especially true for rotor bearings, where the streaks may be seen artfully arranged on the rear of the blades, as demonstrated in figure 27.

Figure 27 Rust streaking to the turbine blades (Ian Woofenden © 2017)

When water moisture has not been a factor, a fine black powder may be seen around the bearing race or on nearby surfaces. This is most often found in protected areas, such as the rear rotor & the yaw bearings inside the turbine nacelle.

Grease/oil where it shouldn't be is a sign that the bearings seals have broken down. Loose hardware can also leave similar signs, when vibration & movement have worn away protective coatings & then oxidation has occurred.

Inspect all turbine-to-tower mounting hardware & check for proper torque. Look for any cracking or other signs of stress to the mainframe welds. Check the integrity of all the blade mountings, including loose blades & any missing hardware. Also, check each of the blades for structural integrity; cracking, pitting, erosion, leading edge wear or any damaged or missing leading edge tape. If excessive movement is found, egging of mounting holes or other damage may be present. Slowly spin the rotor, listening for any unusual noise or a resistance to the turning movement. This can be caused by grit on the magnets, dry bearings, too much play or even the magnets rubbing on the stator. Check for bearing slop by lifting upward on the rotor.

Inspect all the bearing & pivot points. This typically includes all rotor & yaw bearings, furling bearings or pivot, furling or brake assembly & any other friction areas. Check all or any brake pads for wear. Inspect the condition of any flexible hoses in the air brake system & check the colour of any desiccant. The colour changes as moisture is absorbed to indicate when a replacement is needed.

When examining the slip-ring & brush assembly. Look for any pitting or roughness (signs of electrical arcing) & for uneven wear on slip rings. Brushes can jump track or track unevenly causing excessive slip-ring & brush wear, arcing & even premature failure to the assembly. Inside this assembly is the place to look for signs of black dust, metal shavings or excessive grease from bearing failure which can cause electrical problems by interfering with brush contact & the slip rings.

Inspect all the turbine cable connections. Look for signs of wear & any loose terminals caused by vibration, evidence of arcing & check for conductor insulation breakdown. Also be aware that corrosion from moisture may be present inside terminal blocks or any of the other connectors.

Some sealed bearings should be greased with a needle ended grease gun. Any grease seal openings created during this process should be carefully & thoroughly sealed to keep out any moisture. Where applicable, grease all fittings & change gearbox oil according to the manufacturer's recommendations.

As far as your insurance, warranty or guarantee is concerned, they may ask for annual (or bi-annual) inspections by an accredited individual who can certify the integrity of the wind turbine instillation. If however you wish to undertake the inspections yourself & certify the integrity, then it may be advisable to undertake a training course which will allow you to do this. You should not expect to pay around £600 for this sort of training course. It may work out cheaper to undertake the course yourself, rather than pay for a company to check your wind turbine every year.

Chapter 9 - Using a calculator to do the maths

Before you can undertake the calculations in this book, it is important to realise that you would have previously worked similar calculations when you were still at school, therefore it is not anything you have not undertaken previously. Also, now you can use a calculator, will not be marked by a teacher & will use the mathematics to save yourself money. With a little practice, the mathematics will become simple & what could be better than saving yourself money.

All you need to remember is that the letters in the equations are just substituting numbers. They are shown as letters as they are variable. For instance, 30 watts, 3kW, 5kW are all power levels & any could be used in an equation relating to electrical power, therefore a substitute letter is used & you just have to replace that letter for the number. Also, the equations are written back to front, the answer is on the left, the sum is on the right. Therefore you can swap the order if you find it helpful.

Finally, when you have swapped the letters for numbers, calculate from right to left, top, then bottom, working the figures in the brackets first.

In this example from earlier in the book, it is used to find the voltage.

$$V = I \times R$$

If you can remember back to chapter 3,

$$I(amps) = V(volts) \div R(\Omega)$$

So to do the mathematics in this example, just multiply I by R, this will give V (the voltage). If I is 20 & R is 12, the sum will be:

$$V = 20 \times 12$$

The answer is obviously 240 volts. As you can see, there was nothing complicated there & you were most likely able to complete that calculation in your head.

The principles are exactly the same for the more complex equations contained in any electrical cabling equations. Just follow the rules, right to left, top then bottom & substitute the letters for numbers before you start. You may need to use a scientific calculator to do some of these, but again it's just a case of pressing the corresponding buttons. If you do not have a scientific calculator, then you will definitely have one on your computer or even on your mobile phone (if you have a smart phone).

Another example from earlier in the book is to calculate the voltage drop for a single phase AC (or DC) circuit.

$$V_D = I \times \frac{(2 \times L \times R)}{1000}$$

V_D = Voltage Drop in Volts.
I = Cable Current in Amperes.
R = Cable Resistance in Ohms (Ω) (Ω/km).
L = Cable length in meters.

If I is 20 & the length of the cable is 5 meters, then L is 5 (because it is 5 meters). You can obtain the resistance for the cable from charts or from the cable manufacturer. In this instance it is assumed that it has a value of 0.0002, therefore the equation will be as follows:

$$V_D = 20 \times \frac{(2 \times 5 \times 0.0002)}{1000}$$

It is therefore a much simpler matter to calculate the answer. Always start with the brackets.

$$V_D = 20 \times \frac{0.002}{1000}$$

Then divide the top from the bottom.

$$V_D = 20 \times 0.000002$$

Finally multiply the two figures to find the voltage drop (V_D).

The answer is as follows:

$$V_D = 0.00004$$

Therefore the voltage drop will be 0.00004 volts.
Again I'm sure you will agree that was not too difficult, therefore to complete each & every one of the calculations just follow the same rules:

Start with the brackets, work from right to left & top to bottom & substitute the letters for numbers before you start. You will then be able to undertake the calculations with ease & with accuracy if you follow those simple rules.

If you still find these equations a little daunting, then there are calculators freely available on the internet that will calculate the mathematics for you. You can even download suitable calculators onto your tablet or smart phone that will also do the mathematics. There are therefore multiple options available for your calculations.

Chapter 10 - Easing the installation

If you wish to make your life as easy as possible, the first step is to use the correct tool for the job at hand. For instance you can not saw a length of wood with a bread knife, knock in nails with a toffee hammer or secure nuts & bolts with tweezers.

Therefore at the very least you will require a basic tool kit. More specialist tools that will be useful would include the following items:

If working off a ladder is problem, one solution may be to use a **scaffold tower** to help make working at height both easier & safer. There are many heights & widths available & they can be purchased from £600 from a well known auction site in either steel or aluminium. If they are to be used regularly, it may also be advantageous to install wall mounted anchor loops so that it can be securely tied to a wall when it is used against a wall to give access to the roof for checking &/or maintaining any roof mounted PV panels &/or solar hot water panels. If a tower is obtained that is square, it would be suitable to be constructed around a wind turbine's tower, therefore making maintenance far easier than working from a ladder.

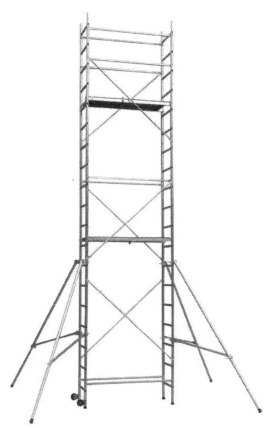

Figure 28 An inexpensive scaffold tower (Public Domain Image © 2017)

The next piece of equipment to consider is a **kill-a-watt meter**. This simply informs you as to how much power an appliance is using. It just plugs into a wall socket & the appliance plugs directly into it. It simply acts as a flow-through meter, measuring the flow of electricity. It is possible to use only one of these meters as they just plug in when you need them. It will therefore be possible to measure how much electricity any electrical appliance is using & therefore help make informed decisions regarding power usage.

You can also then make direct power comparisons when you need to replace an item for a more energy efficient model. These meters are very inexpensive & can be obtained online from £10 each.

Figure 29 Kill-a-Watt meter (Public Domain Image © 2017)

A **multimeter** can measure many things, voltage, current & resistance, therefore it is an invaluable tool to use when installing, checking & maintaining an electrical system. A generic model can be obtained online for as little as £10. They are generally sold complete with probes.

Figure 30 An inexpensive multimeter (Public Domain Image © 2017)

A similar tool is known as a **clamp meter** or a current clamp. It is similar to a multimeter, but is far safer to use as it measures the magnetic field & therefore does not have to make physical contact with the bare metal. Figure 31 shows an inexpensive clamp meter which can be bought online for £25.

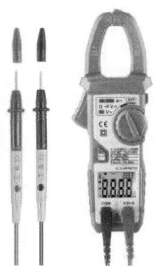

Figure 31 An inexpensive clamp meter (Public Domain Image © 2017)

Both the multimeter & the clamp meter are similar instruments as they both do the same thing, but neither will measure the surge when an electric motor starts. To do this, an expensive multimeter or an expensive clamp meter will need to be purchased, one which can measure a surge. The cheapest available online in the UK can be purchased for approximately £70.

Also, there is a **megohmmeter** to consider. This is a type of ohmmeter that is used to measure the electrical resistance of insulators. Insulating components, for example cable jackets, must be tested for their insulation strength at the time of commissioning & as part of maintenance of high voltage electrical equipment & installations.

For this purpose megohmmeters which can provide high DC voltages (typically in ranges from 500v to 5kV) at specified current capacity are used. This instrument can therefore check your cable runs for ground faults. A typical cheap generic model can be purchased online in the UK for £30.

Figure 32 An inexpensive megohmmeter (Public Domain Image © 2017)

These are not the only tools that are available which will be beneficial. The main piece of equipment that you can use is the **internet** as there are numerous places on the internet that you can get help & advice.

There are numerous chat rooms & forums available where there are lots of helpful people who are more than willing to give advice & pass on the benefit of their wisdom. You only need to ask for help & advice & people from all over the globe will be able to assist you with your own DIY home energy solution. That type of help is priceless.

Chapter 11 – Obtaining finance, grants & mortgages

Hidden benefits from using a CPS installer

If you opt to use one of the approved contractors from the **Microgeneration Certificate Scheme** (MCS) to fit your wind turbine system, then there is a financial benefit as a consequence.

This is the Feed-in Tariffs scheme (FITs) which was designed by the UK Government to be an incentive to the uptake of electricity generating renewable technologies such as solar panels & wind turbines. This means that if you have an eligible installation you could be paid for the electricity you generate as well as for the surplus electricity you export to the grid.

Since 1st April 2010, for installations up to 50kW will need to use an MCS certified installer & an approved technology (which includes wind turbine power installations) to be eligible for FITs. The MCS installer will provide an MCS Certificate once the installation is complete.

To register for the FITs you will then need to send the MCS Certificate to your FIT Licensee (an electricity company) who will complete the registration process. You will then benefit from receiving FITs payments made up of two components (although this is subject to change):

- The generation tariff: your chosen energy supplier will pay you a set rate for each unit (or kWh) of electricity you generate. Once your system has been registered, the tariff levels are guaranteed for the period of the tariff (up to 20 years) & are index-linked.

- The export tariff: our chosen energy supplier will pay you a further rate for each unit you export back to the electricity grid, so you can sell any electricity you generate but do not use yourself. At some stage smart meters will be installed to measure what you export, but until then it is estimated as being 50% of the electricity you generate.

The amount that individuals are paid tends to fluctuate due to whatever government is in power & how keen they are on being seen to be green. Currently (at the time of writing), the upper limits of the tariffs are as follows:

Source	Scale	Tariff (p/kWh)
PV	<10kW	4.07
PV	10 – 50kW	4.29
PV	50 – 250kW	1.94
Wind	<50kW	8.33
Wind	50 - 100kW	4.92
Wind	100 – 1,500kW	2.88
Wind	1,500 – 5,000kW	0.81

It is also important to realise this is the top tier. There is also a medium rate & a lower rate. Which rate you receive will depend on when the installation was commissioned &/or registered.

Whichever tariff is applicable to your individual installation, expect it to change due to the political climate & governmental budget considerations. Currently if the installation has not been installed by a MCS approved contractor or is greater than 50kW, then you can apply through the Roo-FIT scheme via OFGEM. Any electricity you export will be to whichever company operates in your area, as shown in figure 33.

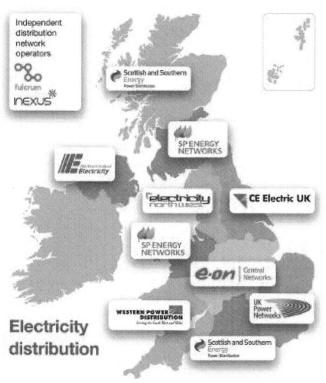

Figure 33 UK distribution network companies (Inexus © 2016)

Renewable Heat Incentive (RHI)

The domestic Renewable Heat Incentive (RHI) for the residential market was launched in 2014, which made a payment (provided you purchase a system they recommend & also use one of their installers) as indicated on the next chart:

Household size	Assumed system size	RHI annual payment 1st Apr 17 – 31st Dec 17
2 person	2m^2	£200
3 person	3m^2	£270
4 person	4m^2	£345
5 person	6m^2	£445
6 person	6m^2	£485

Currently, the RHI will work in a very similar way to Feed-In tariffs. Homeowners will be paid a fee for generating their own hot water using eligible technologies which includes solar thermal water heating panels & collectors. The amount of hot water generated will either be measured or estimated & then you should receive a payment for the total amount created.

Since its inception, the UK government has revised the scheme a number of times. The latest revision was on 20th September 2017 & the guidelines for the current revisions, along with the eligibility requirements & a calculator are available on the internet[19]. Also, currently, the feed in tariffs are tax free for domestic installations, but commercial installations are not. This may well change in the future.

Currently, there are different types of payments that make up the FIT scheme.

The generation tariff (element) rewards you for actually generating electricity. This is estimated from whatever size your system is. For instance, a 4kW system would pay one rate; a 10kW system would pay another rate. The export tariff (element) rewards you for what you actually export from your system into the National Grid system. This element is measured.

---

[19] https://www.ofgem.gov.uk/environmental-programmes/ domestic-rhi/applicants - 30/10/2017

Together, the generation tariff & the export tariff are added together & these are what make up the FIT's payments.

There is also often what is called an 'energy offset' if you look at what the MCS installers quote, but this is just what you could save from your energy bills. Therefore it is best ignored because it is just a way of double counting to make their systems look better than what they are.

Further grants

Currently, the UK government are working towards the EEC's Renewable Energy Directive. This EEC directive sets out a requirement that all EEC members must source 20% of their energy from renewable energy sources by 2020. As the UK is set to withdraw from the EEC, it is impossible to predict exactly how this will affect government grants in the future, but currently, there are sources of income to be made from creating energy from what the government term as renewable energy sources.

Also, as governmental grants & incentives are liable to change, amendment &/or cancelation at any time & sometimes with little or no notice as they move money from one area to another in an attempt to appease various bodies & organisations, it is important to first check on the validity of any information before committing to the expense of any installation.

Grants for wind turbines

In the UK, there are currently no national grants available for installing a wind turbine on domestic or commercial properties.

There are however a small number of regional grants available for 'community wind projects' (ask the 'Sustainability Officer' at your Local Authority for what is available within your area, or in Northern Ireland contact the Bryson Trust[20]), but for domestic & commercial projects the government only offers FIT's payments. There is also a website that lists which grants are available for 'community wind projects' which may be work pursuing if you propose erecting one[21].

The Energy Saving Trust have estimated that as the cost of installing a wind turbine is expensive, the pay back period for the installation may fall outside the lifespan of the turbine. As an example they estimate that a building mounted micro turbine (<2.5kW) may not pay for itself over 20 years. Similarly, a standalone micro turbine (<6kW) may also not pay for itself over a 20 year period. A small standalone (20 -50kW) may take between 8 – 15 years before it becomes profitable & a medium sized turbine (100 – 850kW) could take 7 – 9 years before it becomes profitable.

Only wind turbines <50kW are eligible for FIT's payments, therefore only small micro turbines will be a realistic option for domestic or commercial properties in the UK. Until the UK government starts to issue wind turbine grants, or increases the FIT's payments, micro wind turbines will not be a viable option.

However, if your property is in a remote &/or windy location, it may be possible to make a micro turbine profitable.

Until 2015, there was a small possibility of obtaining a loan to pay for the installation costs for a wind turbine. This was arranged with what was known as the 'Green Deal'. The scheme operated by allowing the loan to be repaid from the savings made from lower electricity bills.

---

[20] https://www.nidirect.gov.uk/contacts/contacts-az/bryson-energy-advice-line

[21]   https://www.renewablesfirst.co.uk/windpower/community-windpower/funding-development-construction/

It may be worth checking periodically for a similar scheme if this type of loan fits your requirements.

In Scotland, 'Home Energy Scotland' can offer a loan of up to £32,500 for owner occupiers to make energy & money saving improvements to their home. This is an interest free loan & is funded by the Scottish Government. It is currently open to new applications from homeowners[22].

As wind turbines >50kW are not eligible for FIT's payments, they are eligible to receive a Renewables Obligation Certificate (ROC) from Ofgem for every MW/h of electricity that they generate. These certificates can then be sold on the open market. Each certificate is (currently) worth approximately £45. It is these ROC payments that make larger turbines more profitable. There are also a number of installers & companies that will pay a set ground rent if you allow them to install a wind turbine at your property. The caveats are that you will need to have land that is suitable for a wind farm & a wind speed that will produce a profitable return. The benefit for the company is that they earn profits from FIT's payments over the lifetime of the installation.

Another option that many installers provide is the option to go 50/50 on the installation, whereby you provide the finance for only half the installation & then get only half the benefits over the 20 or so years that the turbine is in place.

---

[22] http://www.energysavingtrust.org.uk/scotland/grants-loans/home-energy-scotland-loan

Mortgages

You may already know that the word mortgage is a corruption of two French words & translates into English as 'death-grip', but how will an installation of any of the energy saving measures found in this book effect an existing mortgage on property, a remortgage or even a new mortgage for someone wishing to purchase a property that has been outfitted with of any of the energy saving enhancements? This section will therefore address some important questions.

How mortgages can be affected by a wind turbine

As with the 'rent a roof' scheme for PV installations, there is a similar scheme where a company will rent your land & install a wind turbine. As it is essentially the same concept, which is a company installing energy generating equipment for profit, then it is beset with the same problems.

It is therefore important to follow the same advice in the previous pages for PV installations. Therefore, with regard to wind turbines, it would be prudent for any potential purchaser to check on the legality & quality of the installation. This would be good advice to any property purchase whether it is a cash purchase or bought with a mortgage.

The first check would be to ensure whether there is MCS documentation.

If not, proceed with caution. If there is no documentation, it will at least provide an opportunity to reduce the asking price, providing that you are prepared to obtain documentation yourself for the installation if you proceed with the purchase, but if it will be subject to you obtaining a mortgage, you will never get a mortgage on that property due to the lack of documentation & possible conformity.

If however the installation is owned outright, then it should be seen as an asset, as it will provide a modest tax free income for the owner over several years.

It is also advisable to check on the legality of the installation with regard to the Local Authority. If the homeowner can not provide documentation to prove the installation fell within the scope of permitted development when it was first installed, then expect to see documentation either granting Planning Permission or acknowledging it is permitted development. Similarly, expect to see documentation demonstrating compliance with the Building Regulations. If a property owner can not produce any documentation regarding the legality of their installation, it would be best to find another property as the problem of obtaining retrospective Planning Permission &/or retrospective Building Regulation approval is fraught with problems that are best avoided.

Also, if you are planning to install a wind turbine at a property, whether it is a mortgaged property or not, & whether it is a 'rental' scheme or not, it will be in your best interests to ensure that the installation is in complete compliance with all Local Authority Planning conditions & keep all documentation, obtain documentation to prove it falls under Permitted Development (if it is applicable).

Ensure it is built with the Local Authority Building Regulations Approval & keep all documentation to prove it. Ensure it is constructed to all relevant & current standards & that you obtain a MCS Certificate so as to avoid any potential future problems when you sell the property. As these are the requirements that a bank or building society would wish to see & study when assessing a property for the suitability for a mortgage, therefore attempting to buy a property, using a mortgage without this paper trail will at best be problematic, or most usually just rejected.

Also, if the property is leasehold, you may also need the permission of the freeholder.

Table of illustrations

The cover illustration is copyright to Phoenix Xavier (2018).

Figure 1 Simplistic view of the components (P Xavier © 2017) 12

Figure 2 Ohm's law triangle (P Xavier © 2017) 16

Figure 3 Ohm's law 2nd triangle (P Xavier © 2017) 17

Figure 4 Annual average heat from solar radiation (University of Wisconsin © 2016) 22

Figure 5 UK annual average wind speed (Met office © 2011) 23

Figure 6 Buildings creating localised turbulence (P Xavier © 2017) 24

Figure 7 Horizontal axis wind turbine (Patrickmark © 2008) 27

Figure 8 Anatomy of a horizontal axis wind turbine (P Xavier © 2017) 29

Figure 9 Cutaway of a HAWT nacelle & internal components (US Department of Energy © 2014) 30

Figure 10 Darrieus wind turbine (Public Domain Image © 2007) 32

Figure 11 H-Rotor gyromill (Public Domain Image © 2016) 33

Figure 12 Helical Darrieus wind turbine (Anders Sandberg © 2007) 34

Figure 13 Anatomy of a vertical axis wind turbine (P Xavier © 2017) 35

Figure 14 The Bernoulli effect (P Xavier © 2017) 36

Figure 15 Deflection bottle neck (P Xavier © 2017) 39

Figure 16 Air pressure distribution (P Xavier © 2017) 40

Figure 17 Betz Theory power output (P Xavier © 2017) 43

Figure 18 Speed & power output relationship (P Xavier © 2017) 44

Figure 19 How ground structures effect wind speed (P Xavier © 2017) 45

Figure 20 Guyed towers (P Xavier © 2017) 53

Figure 21 Freestanding towers (P Xavier © 2017) 55

Figure 22 Global annual frequency of lightning strikes (Citynoise © 2008) 58

Figure 23 Lightning pole (P Xavier © 2017)...60

Figure 24 Perimeter ground (P Xavier © 2017)..63

Figure 25 Inexpensive Chinese generator (Public Domain Image © 2017)....73

Figure 26 Rusting tie down bolts at tower base (Rust Bullet © 2017).............98

Figure 27 Rust streaking to the turbine blades (Ian Woofenden © 2017).......99

Figure 28 An inexpensive scaffold tower (Public Domain Image © 2017)....106

Figure 29 Kill-a-Watt meter (Public Domain Image © 2017)........................107

Figure 30 An inexpensive multimeter (Public Domain Image © 2017) 107

Figure 31 An inexpensive clamp meter (Public Domain Image © 2017) 108

Figure 32 An inexpensive megohmmeter (Public Domain Image © 2017)...109

Figure 33 UK distribution network companies (Inexus © 2016)....................112

Index

Aberdeenshire 23
AC 12, 59, 103
Aerodynamic Noise 48
Africa 13, 70
Airfoils 33
Altitude 31
Amperage 14
Amperes 14, 58
Amps 14, 15
Anemometer 47, 99
Axis 26
Battery 9, 11, 14, 21, 98
Bearing Wear 31
Bentonite 62
Berkley University 13
Bernoulli Effect 35
Betz' Law 38, 39, 42
Big Infrastructure Group 8
Blackouts 8
Blade Sweep 39
Brake Assembly 28, 100
Bryson Trust 115
Building Regulations 81, 118
    Building Control 81, 82
    Part A 81, 82

Part B 81
Part E 81
Part K 81
Part L 81
Part M 81
Part P 82
Bureaucrats 48
Cairngorm 23
Canada 70
Carrington Event 70
Charge Controller 12, 59, 66, 67, 69
Clamp Meter 87, 107, 108
Community Wind Projects
.... 115
Conductor 15, 64, 67, 101
Conservation Area 78
Cornwall 23
Corrosion 72, 96, 101
Cost Of Electricity 7, 92
County Down 23
Current 14, 15, 16, 18, 19, 20, 65, 68, 69, 82, 87, 88, 107, 108
Cut-in Speed 44
David Cameron 80

DC 12, 59, 103, 108
Degradation 97
Design Life 93
Diesel 74
DTI 47
EEC 8, 74, 114
Eiffel Tower 56
Electric Vehicle 51
Electrical Generator 26
Electricity
   Static Electricity 59
Electricity At Work Act 61
Electromagnetic 69
Electromagnetic Field 66
Electrons 14
EMP 69, 70
Energy
   Electrical Energy . 8, 58, 87
   Heat Energy 11, 17, 21
   Kinetic Energy .. 10, 11, 36, 37, 38, 39
   Light Energy 11
   Solar Energy 10, 11, 83
Energy Efficient 85, 86, 87, 106
Energy Information Administration 7
Energy Saving Trust 115
England 77, 84, 127

Epilepsy 51
Equator 21
Europe 12, 30, 58, 70
Exothermic Weld 61
Feed-In Tariffs 110
   FITs .. 90, 91, 110, 114, 115, 116
Fossil Fuel 7, 9, 21
Freehold
   Freeholder 118
Freestanding Towers 52, 55
Fulminology 57
   Faraday Cage 65
   Gas Discharge Tubes .. 68
   Grounding ... 59, 61, 62, 63, 64, 96, 97
   Lightning 57, 58, 59, 60, 61, 62, 63, 64, 65, 66, 67, 68, 69
   Metal Oxide Varistors ... 68
   Perimeter Ground 62
   Single Point Ground 66, 67
   Skin-Effect 65
   Surge Arrestors 59, 61, 66, 67, 97
   Surge Capacitors 59
   Ufer Ground 63
   Zener Diodes 68
Fuse 81
Galvanic Corrosion 64

Gearbox ... 26, 28, 29, 48, 101

Generator . 28, 29, 31, 36, 48, 59, 73, 74, 75, 76

   Automatic Starter 74

Georges Jean Marie Darrieus 32

Gin Pole 54

Green Alliance 8

Green Deal 115

Guarantee 91, 101

Guy Wires. 53, 54, 55, 56, 64, 95, 96

Guyed towers 53

Heat Cycle 71

Helix 34

Hero of Alexandria 21

Home Energy Scotland . 116

Horizon 92

Hot Air 22

Hot Water 88, 105, 113

   SWH 91

Institute of Mechanical Engineers 8

Inverter 12, 59, 66, 67, 69, 74, 97, 98

James Blyth 21

Kill-a-Watt 85, 88, 106

Lattice Tower 55, 56, 96

Lease

Leasehold 118

LED 86

Listed Building 78

Local Authority .. 51, 80, 115, 118

   Sustainability Officer .. 115

Marconite 63

Mechanical Damage 71

Mechanical Noise 48

Megohmmeter 97, 108

Mehran Moalem 13

Microgeneration Certification Scheme 77, 110

   MCS ... 77, 90, 91, 110, 112, 114, 117, 118

   Roo-Fit 90, 112

Monopole 53, 54, 56

Mortgage 117, 118

Multimeter 87, 97, 98, 107, 108

Nacelle 29, 49, 99

National Grid 7, 10, 21, 30, 57, 69, 76, 90, 113

Newton's Second Law Of Motion 41

North America 30, 70

North Pole 70

Northern Ireland 80, 115

Northern Lights 70

Nuclear 13, 21, 70

OFGEM 112, 116

Ohm's Law 15, 17

Orkney Islands 21

Orography 45

   Roughness Class 46

   Roughness Lengths 46

Permitted Development .. 77, 78, 79, 84, 118

Persia 21

Petrol 8, 74

Photovoltaic 2, 10, 83

Photovoltaic Cells 9

Planning Department . 48, 80

Planning Permission . 77, 78, 79, 80, 118

Power .. 11, 12, 13, 17, 18, 19, 20, 28, 32, 41, 42, 43, 44, 50, 51, 52, 57, 65, 67, 70, 73, 74, 81, 85, 86, 87, 88, 98, 102, 106, 110, 111

Power Coefficient 42

Power Cuts 8, 73, 92

Pressure 14, 22, 35, 36, 37, 40, 41, 66

PV 2, 11, 58, 59, 60, 61, 69, 73, 74, 81, 85, 90, 91, 105, 117

   Roof Mounted ... 51, 52, 90, 105

PVC 72

Rectifier 69

Renewable Energy Directive 114

Renewable Energy Sources 114

Renewable Heat Incentive
   RHI 112

Renewables 13, 114

Renewables Obligation Certificate
   ROC 116

Rent a Roof 117

Resistance 15, 16, 17, 18, 19, 20, 66, 100, 103, 107, 108

Rotor Blades .. 29, 38, 39, 40, 41, 44

Rotor Shaft 26, 28, 30

Rudulf Diesel 74

   BDO 75, 76

   Injector Pump 75

   Positive Displacement Fuel Pump 75

   RDO 75, 76

   SVO 75, 76

   Transesterification 75

   Viscosity 75

   WVO 75, 76

Sahara Desert 13

Scaffold Tower 94, 105

Scheduled Monument 78
Scotland 21, 80, 116
Servo Motor 26
Shadow 28, 51
Short Circuit 68
Shut Down Speed 44
Solar Panel 13, 14, 110
Sound Insulation 49
Standby 87
Sun ... 9, 13, 21, 51, 70, 71, 73
Sunlight 51, 71, 72
Surge Arrestor 66
Temperature ... 15, 22, 37, 47
Tilt Up Tower 54
Torque 32, 34, 36, 98, 100
Turbine Blades 27, 39, 49
Turbulence 27, 28, 31, 41, 45
UK 7, 8, 12, 21, 22, 23, 26, 30, 48, 58, 72, 74, 80, 81, 82, 90, 108, 110, 113, 114, 115
USA 12, 76
UV 71
VAWT 30, 35
Voltage 14, 15, 16, 18, 19, 20, 65, 66, 67, 69, 97, 98, 102, 103, 104, 107, 108
Volts 14, 67, 103, 104
Wales 80

Warranty 91, 93, 94, 101
Water Turbine 11
Weather 22, 72, 90, 93
   Atlantic 23
   Coriolis Force 22
   Jet Stream 23
   Northern Hemisphere .. 22
   Southern Hemisphere .. 22
   Turbulence 24
   Wind Speed . 22, 23, 24, 97
Wind Farm
   Off shore 26
   On Shore 26
Wind Resistance 27
Wind Sensor 26
Wind Shear 28, 54
Wind Speed ... 28, 31, 36, 41, 42, 43, 44, 45, 46, 47, 48
Wind Turbine ... 2, 11, 12, 21, 26, 30, 33, 34, 35, 36, 38, 39, 41, 43, 47, 48, 49, 50, 51, 58, 61, 62, 63, 66, 67, 69, 73, 74, 77, 78, 79, 80, 81, 85, 91, 92, 93, 94, 96, 99, 101, 105, 110, 114, 117, 118
   Darrieus Wind Turbine. 32
   Eggbeater Turbine 32
   Flicker Effect 51
   HAWT 26, 28, 29, 30, 31
   Helical Darrieus Wind
      Turbine 34

Horizontal Axis Wind
    Turbines 26
H-Rotor Gyromills 33
Savonius Rotor 32
VAWT 26, 30, 31, 35
Vertical Axis Wind
    Turbine 28
Vertical Axis Wind
    Turbines 26, 30, 31

Wind Vane 26, 99
Windmills 21
World Energy Demand 7
Yaw Control 28
Zenith 51

About The Author

Mr Xavier is in his 40's & currently living in the South of England. He is desperately trying to make a living, live a good life, learn to play the ukulele, grow a rather splendid handlebar moustache & decide what to have for dinner tonight. With his other hand he's trying desperately to learn another language whilst also planning the next chapter of his life.

This & his other books are available from online booksellers.

Made in the
USA
Columbia, SC